film: the creative eye

BY DAVID A. SOHN

Geo. A. Pflaum, Publisher, Dayton, Ohio 45402

Films discussed here
distributed by Pyramid Films,
Box 1048,
Santa Monica, California 90406

Book Design: Dan Johnson

Observation and creativity are crucial concerns of a relevant education. If we learn to observe accurately and to interpret what we see imaginatively, the effect upon our academic performance and human growth can be immense.

These themes have been a preoccupation of mine for several years. My first work in the use of visual stimuli to train observation and to increase verbal facility was in collaboration with Hart Day Leavitt of Andover on the book, *Stop, Look and Write*. Since then, two other books, *The Writer's Eye* (by Leavitt) and *Pictures For Writing* (by Sohn), have been published forming what is called the *Stop, Look and Write Series*. Each of these books is a program which uses visual stills (pictures, cartoons, paintings, and drawings) to increase observational skills in relation to writing, discussion, and reading.

I mention these books because they are initial steps in a learning program for visual literacy, and they relate to many of the ideas in this book. A logical and exciting extension of the visual technique was the use of the short film as a work of art that contains little or no narration—films of few words. During my last year as a teacher in the classroom in Darien, Connecticut, I used about 70 films in conjunction with the *Stop, Look and Write* program to test out this idea. The results were more than gratifying. My classes were the most enthusiastic of my career, but even more rewarding was the increased proficiency of the verbal behavior of students who were learning to observe, discuss and write.

Ours is an age in which the study of processes in our environment is much more important than the accumulation of facts. Marshall McLuhan observes: "Environments are invisible. Their ground rules, pervasive structures, and overall patterns elude easy perception." A vivid example of this observation is the sudden awareness of pollution throughout the nation. It has always been with us, but only recently have we observed its dangers. Fred Friendly's suggestion that "what we don't know may kill us" seems particularly appropriate.

The themes of developing observation and creativity are fundamental to this book, but it also contains insights into the art of filmmaking that serve as counterpoints from the practicality of the firing line rather than from the foggy realm of theory. You will notice that all of the films in the book are made or distributed by Pyramid Films in Santa Monica. I had the opportunity of interviewing the people who created these films during a month I spent in Santa Monica. The dimension that these interviews add to the book is invaluable. Also, over the years I have been impressed with Pyramid's high standards of quality, and their films fit perfectly with the kind of program I wanted to design.

I am grateful to all the people who cooperated in this venture, which was, for me, an adventure. I am particularly grateful to my wife for tolerating grumpiness, odd hours and all the writer's faults, and to Lynn and David Adams for their vast amount of help.

I hope that teachers and students who use this program will find their experiences as delightful as the experience of writing and creating it was for me. Once you set your sights, the field of vision expands.

The interviews with Saul Bass were tape-recorded during two separate sessions. The tapes were later transcribed and somewhat edited. They are not intended to be polished, or careful pieces of writing. The same applies to the other interviews in this book.

David A. Sohn
Evanston, Illinois, 1970

CONTENTS

"How . . . do we arouse the child's interest in the world of ideas? Several tentative recommendations have already been made in the spirit of suggesting needed research. Principal among these were increasing the inherent interest of materials taught, giving the student a sense of discovery . . ."

—Jerome Bruner, *The Process of Education,* ©1962, Harvard University Press.

"To see or to perish is man's condition. To see more is to become more. Fuller being means closer union."

—de Chardin

"The task I'm trying to achieve is, above all, to make you see."

—D. W. Griffith

INTRODUCTION

The art of seeing, the power of observation — whatever you label the skill of probing and understanding the world that surrounds you — the mastery of such skill, is one of the most important goals of learning. Developing sensory awareness, the searching eye, the precise ear, the sensitive touch, the detecting nose, the discriminating tongue, combine to form the "compleat man," the self-educating, curious enigma that sees the world in a grain of sand or the camel in the cloud.

In a changing, increasingly complex world, our senses are bombarded incessantly by a shower of images. Unless we learn to observe our environment, to reach some understanding of it, we succumb to it, blinded and stupefied by the slush of media wash.

By placing aspects of the environment in another medium such as a book, record, painting, or film we can observe them better, without distraction. Eliminating the total context that camouflages the significant, we isolate an important element from the total scene. Then we can observe it clearly. The writer, the composer, the artist, the filmmaker, all serve us by making the invisible, visible. Like magicians, they manipulate the environment with their media. The waste of the vastland is eliminated through the artist's sharper vision.

The power of observation involves all the senses. We do not see with merely our eyes or hear with our ears alone. We observe with the total sensorium.

The invention of the modern camera in 1835 was a tremendous breakthrough. The still photograph is a moment in time, a piece of the action preserved. Photographs have been called by Norman Mailer "data points — crystals of memory to give emotional resonance to experience . . ." Photographs have tremendous power to inspire observation, discussion, writing. The photographer composes with visual language as the writer composes with verbal language. Each medium has a singular impact, an integrity of its own. The poet, the novelist, the essayist, can move us or bore us. The photographer of genius can jolt our imaginations with images, or underexpose us with a cliché. The master of any medium awakens us with his fresh perceptions. Each is an artist through his special vision.

The motion picture film is a kinetic catalyst, a moving composition. It creates an environment in another dimension, yielding an illusion of reality. As the film artist creates and composes with craft and skill, he edits and splices life as he perceives it. Compressing and juggling time, space and matter, using sound and silence to complement and enhance visual experience, the film artist captures his world in the grain of celluloid. When he succeeds, he reels you in. As the reel revolves, the film involves. His art is a metaphor for the eyes, for all the senses — a moving mirage that reflects upon us, that we reflect upon. His finest perceptions change us, sometimes profoundly. Through his creative eye, his sensitivity and sensibility, he renews us, by showing us what we never knew. As Marshall McLuhan once said, "the filmmaker is Cyclops, the hunter." He searches, captures, and creates a world we have never seen or experienced. He shares his sense of discovery through his finest work, the liberating art of film.

THE SHORT FILM

Creators of short films are much like poets. Their eyes are not on large commercial markets. They *have* to make their films, as a poet *has* to write a poem. The main satisfaction is in the realization of the creative impulse.

As a consequence, short films are fresh and vital, often experimental in nature. Their techniques and conceptions are actually the DEW-line of filmmaking. They add, and continue to add, to the grammar of the film. Free of commercial constrictions, the experimental filmmaker fearlessly tries new ideas, new techniques. He unconsciously leads the pack, unwittingly needling the sluggish dinosaur of Hollywood.

The excellent short film is both powerful and practical. It's very different from the dreary instructional film that leads you, step by step, down the stairs of stifling stupor. (*How to Build a Birdhouse, A Trip to the Sanitation Plant, How To Be a Successful Date,* for example). The finest of short films are brief, involving experiences that stand the test of repeated viewing. When there is narration, the words support the images.

They do not intrude. Often, there is no narration. The camera carries the message through visual language and a fresh sound track. Skillful editing and a variety of images take you along with rhythm and visual excitement, resulting in a thematic impact that lingers and satisfies. Such films add to your perception and understanding of the environment, entertaining as well as educating. They succeed by creating a new awareness, a fuller sense of life and being.

Short films are timely, unlike some features which are apt to become dated before they are released, due to the fact that the grammar of film is growing and changing rapidly. Short films are generally conceived, created, and released quickly, in months, rather than years, as is the case with many features. Consequently, short films seem more contemporary.

THE PROGRAM:

For centuries, books have been springboards to learning—to discussion, to writing, to contemplation. This tradition suffers only from its limitations. The printed word and the spoken word remain the major media of convenient communication. Yet so much more is available that can stimulate and expand experience. Media such as recordings, television, filmstrips, posters, radio, the film—all can create rich and relevant environments resulting in deeper probes and broader experiences. Print will not disappear, nor should it, but the sense of discovery depends on the complete spectrum, the total picture, the full and fulfilled vision.

The premise of this book, then, is that visual literacy is becoming increasingly important. So much of our experience is concerned with visual and auditory impacts. We must cope with the clever slanting of advertising, the mosaic of television and radio, and the reel world of the movie theater.

"In innumberable ways, if we are rigid, dogmatic, arrogant, we shall be laying stone upon stone, an ugly thing . . . The educator can be the withholder as well as the giver of life."

—Loren Eiseley, *The Mind as Nature,*
© 1962. Harper & Row, Publishers, Inc.

Film:
The Creative Eye
a sense of
discovery

"Who placed us with eyes between a microscopic and telescopic world? I have the habit of attention to such excess that my senses get no rest, but suffer from a constant strain."

—Henry David Thoreau

"All we know, we acquire—observing, exploring, experiencing."

—From the film, *The Searching Eye*

I. THE SEARCHING EYE: The Observer and the Creative Spirit

THE SEARCHING EYE

WHY MAN CREATES

The Searching Eye and *Why Man Creates,* inter-relate as an overview on observation and creativity. The concepts developed will be helpful in understanding all other films described in this book.

THE SEARCHING EYE

A film produced by Saul Bass & Associates for the Eastman Kodak Company.

Conceived and designed by Elaine and Saul Bass.

Directed by Saul Bass. Narration written by Paul David.

Lion of St. Mark (Grand Award) — Venice International Children's Film Festival.

Time: 18 min.; Color

Distributed by Pyramid

One of the secrets of making a successful film, especially when it contains narration, is to avoid preaching. Sermons belong to the domain of religion. Great books, speeches, and films imply themes, but they do not hammer the participant with obvious blows. As a famous Hollywood mogul put it, "If I want a message, send me a telegram."

Elaine and Saul Bass could easily have failed with this film, but their wisdom and taste kept the delicate balance between visual impact and narration. The narration is economical, and precisely developed. The filmmakers wisely space the words. Narration occurs as progressive islands, while the camera tells most of the story. As a constructive design, the narration alone is an object lesson for anyone who wants to learn to write a script or a tightly developed composition.

The story is a simple one as a surface plot. A ten-year-old boy goes to the beach to see what he can see. He explores a pool and is nipped by a crab. He swims underwater. He drops a rock on the beach, chases and imitates birds. He finds a piece of sheet music on the beach and uses it as a flag for the sand castle he builds. He inhabits it with toy soldiers. His imagination then takes over and there is a battle of ancient knights, broken only by waves that destroy his reverie. A still photographer takes his picture. He eats an apple and drops a seed on the beach. After a pleasant day, he heads for home.

As the film ends, the boy has seen much, but it is what he cannot see that adds a profound dimension to the film. As the simple story unfolds, the unseen world is interjected periodically through the searching eye of experience and knowledge that the boy lacks. The film begins with close-ups of eyes — a baby eagle, a gorilla, an owl, a parrot, a chick, and finally the eye of the boy. All of the animals have complex, sensitive, efficient eyes, but they observe only the present. They are not concerned with the past, they are unmindful of the future. Only man realizes that he is a temporary guest on this planet — that he someday will die. As the film states, the eye of man is "a simple tool for measuring, a complex instrument for the contemplation of the unknown, the mysterious, the beautiful."

3

Yet as wonderful as the eye of man may be, the camera, an extension of his own eyes, enables him to see much more. His eyes cannot penetrate conveniently the darker reaches of the sea, but the camera does it for him as we see creatures of the deep on the screen.

Throughout the film, the simple actions of the boy lend the opportunity for the visual metaphors of the normally unseen world. When he drops a rock on the beach, the camera shows the "constructive violence and destructive beauty" of volcanic eruptions in the past that no human eye could see in the same way. As the boy chases birds and imitates them, we see that "imitation is the beginning of learning." Man's attempt to fly with wings is superimposed over the flight of a bird. As gulls glide to the left, a matching shot of fighter planes is superimposed behind the birds. The grace of flight is caught with a shot of a bird through slow-motion, stroboscopic photography.

The sand castle affords an opportunity to investigate the inner eye. "All men are gifted with the alchemy of sight—the power of seeing one form in the shape of another—of bringing objects to life in the eye of the imagination." He builds the castle. The boy watches the fierce battle among the knights in the castle as it takes place in his imagination. It ends with the abrupt rush of a wave. The sand castle is the boy's creation. "Where once there was nothing, he builds and gives reality to his vision." As the tide proceeds to wreck his creation, the narration states: "Man struggles to preserve his vision and his dreams. Man recognizes the strength of reality. He accepts it and becomes part of it." The boy joins the force of nature in destroying his creation.

As he searches for a more perfect perception of reality, we see a slow-motion shot of a drop of water, the splash becomes a crown, and the action is frozen in a symmetrical image of great beauty. The apple seed on the beach introduces the metaphor of growth. We see strawberries ripen through time-lapse photography. We see poppies open, a stunning multiple screen sequence of blooming roses, and then a hollyhock magnificently unfolds.

"Knowledge has no boundaries," says the narrator. "The horizons are ever receding. The more we are able to see, the more we look for. The more we question, the more we need to question. The more we contemplate, the greater the need for contemplation. His vision, aided by the searching eye of the camera, penetrates into the further regions of the universe."

Throughout this sequence, we see telescopic shots of a sunset, fire-storms on the sun, and distant galaxies.

The film ends with one of the great receding shots in the cinema. Beginning with a close-up of the boy, the camera gradually moves backward and upward (on a helicopter) until we see vast fields, and the boy becomes a speck on a distant path. As it moves, we hear these words: "For there is so much to see, so much to learn, so much to know. And the promise of knowledge and beauty is the reward of the searching eye."

The story, then, is more than the day of a young boy on the beach. Simple instances are juxtaposed with the dazzling capabilities of the camera. A wide variety of cinematographic techniques are used. "The camera slows down the truth so we can see . . . the camera speeds up the truth. Our vision is enriched so we can see and understand." Microphotography shows us the inner world. Telescopic photography shows us worlds beyond our grasp. The ending of the film foreshadows exploring the moon's surface, Mars, and the universe. In addition to developing the themes of observation, perception and imagination, *The Searching Eye* serves as a primer of film technique that should be seen several times to appreciate the ingenuity of its construction, the sensitivity of its techniques, and the profundity of its impact.

MAKING THE FILM:

The original format of the film was an interchange of 35mm and 70mm projection. Because of the nature of the conversion to 16mm projection, some of the wide-screen qualities do not appear in this version. This factor does not diminish the impact of the film to any significant extent because special processing and re-shooting enabled the 16mm reduction to retain many of the optical effects of the original.

The film frequently employs a split-screen image and as many as four simultaneous images on a divided screen (in the flowering sequence). Also employed by the Bass organization are aerial photography, underwater photography, extreme slow-motion (the drop of water), time-lapse photography, freeze-frame shots, micro-photography, stroboscopic photography (the slow-motion flying bird), and telescopic photography.

Fifty boys were screened by the Bass organization before Walter Lane was selected to play the part. He had no previous acting experience.

Fifteen cameramen shot 25,000 ft. of film before it was edited into its present form.

The music was especially composed and conducted by Jeff Alexander. Victor Perrin narrated the film.

6

AFTER THE FILM:

1. What might life be like without sight? Helen Keller's essay, "Three Days to See," would help you think about this.
2. What can the camera do that the eye cannot do? Look at the film a second time with this question in mind. Discuss the various film techniques you notice.
3. What do you think about the statement in the film: "All we know, we acquire—observing, exploring, experiencing"? Maybe you recall a dramatic personal experience in which you learned by the jolt of the experience, as the boy did with the crab.
4. Create a collage or a thematic visual poster which will illustrate the importance of observation.
5. If you have a camera, could you photograph some aspect of the environment that you could not experience with your eye?
6. What are some instances where keen observation can be crucial?
7. As you examine magazines, you might notice photographs that are the works of a particularly perceptive eye. What qualities make the photographs special? Could you write about them as examples of sharp observation and visual composition?

SAUL BASS

Saul Bass is a graphic and industrial designer as well as a filmmaker. His short films have won many awards, among them an Oscar for *Why Man Creates*. He is also known for his work with theatrical motion pictures including his Epilogue for *Around the World in Eighty Days*, his direction and editing of the racing scenes in *Grand Prix* and his Prologues for *Man with the Golden Arm, Walk on the Wild Side* and *It's a Mad, Mad, Mad, Mad World*. Saul Bass and his associates are also responsible for the package design of numerous products such as Wesson Oil, the Dixie Cup line and Kleenex tissues. His organization has also developed visual communications programs for major companies including Alcoa, Celanese and AT&T.

THE SEARCHING EYE

SOHN: Mr. Bass, what are some of the problems you encountered when you conceived *The Searching Eye?*

SAUL BASS: I was concerned with how it is possible for one to perceive an event that has been experienced many, many times—that is totally familiar and cause it to become unfamiliar. How do you make the event *seen* for the first time? It's easy to deal with exotic material and make it interesting . . . say Balinese temples. But how do you make an ordinary church elicit the same level of interest and intensity of focus, going in, as would occur if there were a Balinese temple on that site? . . .

In *The Searching Eye,* that was the problem I set for myself. There's beauty in the most ordinary things if they are perceived within a certain framework. The most beach-like beach was the one I was looking for—the most wave-like waves, the most bird-like birds . . .

Everything in the film was approached from that point of view—to take the ordinary, unexotic expressions of these things and find a way of looking at them that would reveal the known as an unknown . . .

I remember reading about Mozart traveling to Rome from Vienna. Upon arrival in Rome, he was asked, "What did you think of the Alps?" He answered, "What Alps? . . ." We all go through a process of filtering what we see . . .

The film dealt with two sets of phenomena. A child goes through his environment and there are things he sees and certain other things he doesn't, or cannot, see. The boy is aware of one set of phenomena that he can directly perceive . . . But there is another set that he will not perceive at this moment in his life. He cannot see what is in the ocean, or at microscopic or cosmic levels . . . he doesn't know the history of the earth . . .

The film, as omnipotent observer, shows us, the audience, the phenomena that the boy cannot see. It also allows the audience to enter the boy's mind . . . his imagination . . .

SOHN: Were there any pitfalls that you had to be wary of when you made the film?

BASS: Yes, there are certain traps you have to avoid when you talk about "seeing," in relation to a child . . . for example, the common conception of the "child-like eye." We have a tendency to say that the untutored mind has an intuitive capacity to perceive beauty and that somehow or other we destroy that capacity when observation becomes more sophisticated. I don't believe this is so.

We also talk about the "primitive eye." Gauguin is partially responsible for the myth of the "untutored savage" who supposedly has a clearer eye, a greater sense of beauty, and a greater ability to perceive beauty in phenomena. It's not true. The untutored, primitive eye is as incompetent as the untutored eye in any civilization.

I collect primitive artifacts. There is as much ugly work done in this area as there is beautiful work. It always depends upon the quality of the artist. If the theory were true, everything observed or produced in these primitive cultures would be more beautiful . . . to some degree. It isn't. The woods were as full of bad art in those days as they are now.

Primitive eyes have no greater sense of beauty than our own untutored eyes have. Children don't have intrinsic good taste. You have to develop a sense of taste.

One quality that children often do have is this — they are not impeded by false notions of what is good or bad . . . and as a result have decent intuitive notions of what constitutes appropriate form.

SOHN: What do you mean by the term "beauty," Mr. Bass?

BASS: For me, the term "beauty" is synonymous to "appropriate form." An "appropriate form" may be a visual configuration which is either disturbing or pleasant. But if it is appropriate to the nature of what it is, it is "beautiful" whether it is a found object or a created object.

There has been much confusion in our time between innovation and quality. It has been characteristic to say, "Look! Mary made this lamp out of driftwood. And John made this piece of furniture. Isn't that wonderful?" Now, it isn't wonderful. It's probably terrible! . . . He should have gone out and bought a good piece of furniture. This may be very good for John as a therapeutic experience. But that doesn't make it "good." It only makes it useful to John.

I had to arrive at what was legitimate for the boy to see — what was valuable in this process of seeing, for him as well as for ourselves. I had to arrive at what would be true, without introducing a false sentimentality about what a child is capable of seeing . . .

SOHN: I was impressed with the sand castle. Did you face any problems in that sequence?

BASS: I'm a practiced sand castle builder. Some of the most magnificent ones you can imagine are strewn along the beaches of the Atlantic, washed into the sand, where I grew up.

One problem was to build a sand castle that would be believable for the child to build. I kept the castle relatively simple. It might easily have become exotic, but I had to control that tendency.

SOHN: How did you animate the soldiers in the battle sequence?

BASS: The figures were all animated by simple motion below the bottom frame of the camera. We simply moved them and turned them. We had them on sticks and little turntables that were operated by string. As I pushed them in, I could pull the string, and that would unwind them. When a knight came through with an axe, it looked like he was swinging it when he unwound. It was very simple.

In other cases, we would just stand them up and stay out of camera range. We used a little stick at the appropriate moment to knock them over. We had a lot of people around with little sticks, everybody hitting things. It was a lot of fun. We enjoyed that.

SOHN: How did you get the waves to behave so well?

BASS: We built temporary retaining walls. We simply took four-by-eights of plywood, drove some stakes into the beach, and put the plywood in front of the stakes. We couldn't get the impact any other way. The plywood formed a sort of semi-arc around the castle, which was about five to eight feet away. This kept the waves from hitting it directly. A wave would go around it or sweep up behind, but it didn't do too much damage there.

We would wait for a big wave. Not every wave has the same strength. The difficulty was to make a judgment as to whether a big one was coming in or not. I couldn't wait until the wave was on top of the boards, because it took us so many seconds to get the boards out. I had to decide when the wave was just forming. If I signalled at that point, we could get the boards out in time for the wave to come through to the castle.

I would yell for them to pull the boards, and if it was a small one, it destroyed the castle but it didn't give us the effect. If it was a big one, it did what we wanted it to do.

SOHN: You must have used a lot of castles?

BASS: We built a series of castles on the beach. We had molds made. After I finished my first castle out at Santa Monica, we made impressions of it and built wooden molds. We would turn the mold upside down, fill it with sand, pound it, put it right side up, then unscrew the sides, pull them off, and that was the castle.

After we set up the castle, I would "trim" it. While I'd be doing that, we'd have a crew setting up another castle about five or eight feet further up the beach, because the tide would be coming in then. I'd be shooting on the one castle and let the wave through. If it didn't work, we'd go on to the next castle, where the waves were beginning to build up. That would give us another half hour to set up and do some extra shots. By that time, we were ready to try the next castle. At one time, we had about seven castles strung along the beach. I guess we did it about 15 or 20 times, before we got the whole thing worked out. It became somewhat tedious. It looks very spontaneous, but as is always the case in these matters, it takes a considerable amount of planning, patience, care, and time.

SOHN: Were there other problems?

BASS: There was the crab sequence. We were shooting the boy and the crab out on a tidal shelf, an isolated flat of rock, and it was medium tide. The tide started to come in and we had to finish the shot, so we wound up in water up to our waists, and the camera was just above the water. Walter, the boy, was on dry land, but we had started the shot from that position and we couldn't change the angle. Finally, as the tide came in, it was hard to keep the camera from lifting and floating off the bottom. We finally got the shot, stopped, and they had to send a boat out for us.

SOHN: The boy, Walter, does a remarkable job in the film. How did you get such a performance from a boy that young?

BASS: Walter had never acted before, but he came from an acting family. It was, I think, for Walter, an extremely interesting experience. When you work with child actors, it's not only difficult for the director, but it's also extremely difficult for the child. The discipline of making a film is a severe discipline. You have to work very hard. You have to do many "takes" of the same action. The action has to be repeated many times, sometimes without variation, sometimes with certain requested variations. All this takes an enormous amount of concentration and an enormous amount of motivation. Children rarely have that about filmmaking. We ask a child to be an adult. It's unfair to the child.

11

Although many child actors have very serious problems, I think for Walter it was a very good experience because he eventually became quite interested in the whole thing. He learned that summer what it was to do a man's work. That's what it boils down to, and I think it was therefore an extremely valuable experience for Walter. I think it's an exciting thing for a child to get the smell of what it's like to be disciplined, to work hard, do it well and measure up to a standard. Then, he should go back to being a child again, as opposed to what many child actors have to do—to function in a life-sense as adults, when they should be children.

My wife, who collaborates with me on many film projects, worked closely with Walter. In the film, I was using long lenses heavily, which meant that the camera had to be very far from the boy. He needed a good deal of special handling, because he was just a child. A rapport had to be developed between him and myself, and eventually between Elaine and the boy. She wound up working with him, and I directing the camera. She played a very important role.

SOHN: How long did it take to make the film?

BASS: It's very hard to say how long it took. We didn't go right through to the end. We did a bit here, then stopped and did something else. Then did another section, then something else. Then we edited and stopped. It extended over a period of a year—a little over a year.

SOHN: The final shot is very impressive. How did you do it?

BASS: We just started with a zoom lens on the boy's eye, pulled back the zoom lens, and in the middle of the "zoom back," the copter took off and then the rest of the opening up of the view was the actual motion of the copter pulling away.

SOHN: All of your films are rich contributions to education. What are some of your thoughts about the education of youth in today's world?

BASS: Education is accumulated experience of a certain kind. I suppose the implications for education are to help the child see that there are multi-levels upon which phenomena can be experienced. For instance, we're aware that objects no longer simply have volume or weight — they also have texture, feel, and scale. It is as much an experience to experience the size of something as it is to experience its form, or the touching of it, or its color. In the observation of things, it's important to explore all the dimensions, all the possibilities.

Left to its own devices, the untutored eye will tend to reach for a variety of meanings. It will reach in natural, healthy ways. We want to grow towards the sun, not away from it. We want to know more, not less. We want to try more, not less.

So if we leave it alone, it is bound to turn out better than if we tamper with it in the wrong way. If we can help it grow, that is teaching in the best sense of the word. Sometimes, however, the most valuable contribution that teaching can make is to clear things out of the child's way, so that he can get at it directly.

The reason a child's drawing or a child's observation is important, or "good," is because it is
his. The most important experiences that children can have are their own experiences.

When a child makes a mask, we say, "it's a good
mask," especially if it's a mask he has never
made before. It represents a new experience.
The accumulation of new experiences and possibilities are what constitute growth in the child.
So we say, "Everything a child does is good,
everything he sees is good, unless he's restrict-
ing himself." As long as he keeps seeing new
things, doing new things, and trying different
things in looking, seeing, experiencing, thinking—we say, "good, good, good, good!"

When one is an adult, we apply other criteria.
We start to raise questions of appropriateness,
and that makes it another ball game. Are we
interested in teaching children to think and to
function in a creative interaction with their environment, or do we want to teach them to have
a bundle of things and information "bits" that
they can trot out at command and that may or
may not be relevant?

It is becoming increasingly evident that this lat-
ter point of view is less and less viable because
the kinds of problems that will be placed before
them when they are working members of adult
society are unpredictable at this point. Society
is changing so rapidly that we no longer know
what to teach students, because we don't know
what they are going to have to do. What they
will have to do will unquestionably be vastly
different from what has to be done today.

It seems important to develop a flexible, open,
ruminative, discursive, creative ability to look
at a condition and find a relationship to it in a
very individual and special way.

If students don't have this quality, they will grow
up in their world with a set of skills that they
cannot use, with information that is outdated
before they have the opportunity to use it.

It is difficult to be creative, whether you are
teaching or making a film. It is the hardest thing
to do. It hurts! Those who talk about the joy of
creating are talking about something that I don't
understand. There may be satisfactions, joy in
the results, joy momentarily, but in process
mainly painful. Athletes don't talk about "joy"
when they are running a race, because they get
sharp shooting pains up through the lungs. The
joy of athletic activity is in the sense of achievement, of having pushed yourself to the limit, of
discovering that you can perform those tasks
you set for yourself.

13

This is part of what is peculiarly human about
humanity. But talk about joy is nonsense. It
hurts, it is hard work, and I am very appreciative
of that fact when it involves teachers, writers,
filmmakers, or anybody concerned with creativity.

WHY MAN CREATES

A film by Saul Bass made for the
Kaiser Aluminum and Chemical
Corporation.

Written by Saul Bass and Mayo Simon

Academy Award ("Oscar")—
Academy of Motion Picture Arts
and Sciences
Gold Hugo (Grand Award)—Chicago
International Film Festival
Gold Medal (Grand Award)—New
York International Film & TV
Festival
Golden Gate Award (Grand Award)—
San Francisco International Film
Festival
Gold Medal (Grand Award)—Moscow
International Film Festival
Gold Medal—Venice XII Gold
Mercury Film Prize
Grand Award: Festival (Waterford
Glass Award)—Cork International
Film Festival
     Grand Award: Short Films
Gold Camera Award—U.S. Industrial
Film Festival—Chicago
Grand Award: Festival—Berlin X
International Film Festival
     Grand Award: Category
Grand Prix—Nyon (Switzerland)
International Festival
Silver "Osella"—Venice XX
International Exhibition of
Documentary Films
Cindy (Grand Award)—Information
Film Producers of America
Blue Ribbon Award—New York
American Film Festival
Best Screenwriting Award—
Vancouver, B.C., International Film
Festival
Special Jury Prize (Seal of Trieste)—
Trieste (Italy) 7th International
Festival
Golden Eagle Award—Council on
International Non-Theatrical Events

Time: 25 min.; Color

Distributed by Pyramid

"As the dead man is spiritualized, so the imagination requires a long range. It is the faculty
of the poet to see present things as if also past
and future; as if distant or universally significant."

—Henry David Thoreau

"The ability to relate and to connect, sometimes
in odd and yet in striking fashion, lies at the
very heart of any creative use of the mind, no
matter in what field or discipline."

—George J. Seidel, *The Crisis of Creativity*
©1966, University of Notre Dame Press.

"The creative process is often an unpredictable, desperate, yet disciplined kind of activity . . . it has the discipline of order, but the guts of what happens come from other well-springs.

" . . . I think that the statements made in this film are really true . . . in terms of how the creative process feels . . . of how society tends to view the creative guy . . . of the importance of what he does in spite of society's general tendency to reject . . . I don't fault the attitude of society . . . I merely describe it . . . Society has good reason to be reluctant to accept new ideas. Many new ideas are impractical or dangerous. But some of them are the ones that advance society, make it move ahead, make it come to grips with things it has to understand or solve in order to survive and grow . . . But new ideas, somehow or other, continue to be presented because of the peculiar nature of creative people . . .

"Imagination is one of the glorious aspects of humanity . . . it is what makes humans human, rather than animals . . ."

—Saul Bass

To tackle the nature of the creative process presents a number of formidable problems for even the most ingenious minds. Many fine thinkers, including some of our best philosophers, psychologists, and artists, have written about the enigma of the creative person. Until recently, however, there has been no adequate film about the subtleties and mysteries of creativity, except for the intriguing portrait of the producer in Fellini's film, "8-1/2."

Why Man Creates is another remarkable achievement of Saul Bass. What is extraordinary, too, is that although the film was made for Kaiser Aluminum and Chemical Corporation, the company's name is not mentioned in the film until the final credits. The wisdom of this omission speaks well for Kaiser, and could serve as a model for other sponsored industrial films. Most viewers resent commercial intrusion in an otherwise superior film. If the film works, chances are that they will be grateful for the experience and want to know who made it possible.

Why Man Creates, like *The Searching Eye,* is an expertly designed film that combines humor, satire, and irony with serious questions about the well-springs of the creative person. It is described at the outset as a series of explorations, episodes, and comments on creativity. As the film unfolds, it becomes clear that it is precisely these things—a series of probes attempting to answer the question, Why does man create? The film is organized into eight major sections:

1. The Edifice—a fast-moving, frequently ironic overview of the world man has built for himself over the centuries through his political and philosophical ideas and his expanding technological expertise.

16

2. Fooling Around: Sometimes Ideas Start That Way—a section that "fools around" with brilliant special effects in a series of spoofs on incubation, scientific jargon, red tape, conformity, foolish youth, nonconformity, and the vacuous preaching of the older generation. It shows how the artist manipulates reality, and ends with the thought that a creative idea may emerge from apparently useless activity.

3. The Process—a section that depicts a seemingly whacky artist constructing a wild piece of mechanical sculpture. Statements from Edison, Hemingway, and Einstein are injected at intervals to balance the humor with the personal observations of men who were considered, at certain times in their lives, to be far-out eccentrics.

4. The Judgment—a section where the public judges the artist's work harshly. Symbolically he defends his work and attempts to shoot down the critics. In turn he is shot down by them, an all-too-frequent experience for the creative artist.

5. A Parable—here, a non-conformist ball appears, then disappears, leaving the mystery of various interpretations about its disappearance.

6. A Digression—a conversation between two snails which shows that without faith in the germ of an idea, creativity can be squelched by those who do not think.

7. The Search—a series of interviews with creative scientific researchers that illustrates the necessity for long-term commitment to a creative problem and the uncertainty of success. It shows the agony and sweat that the serious creative person must endure. It shows also how the creative person works toward a goal, ignoring time.

8. The Mark—although this section is not labelled as such in the film, here the common threads of connection among creative people of the past and present are suggested. The film ends with an eloquent statement on the unique quality, and implied potential, of the individual.

A NOTE ON USING THE FILM WITH GROUPS:

Why Man Creates is a rich and subtle film which improves with frequent viewing. It should be screened at least twice. A discussion of the creative process before the first showing might deepen understanding. Among worthwhile questions to consider are: What qualities does a creative person have? How would you describe creativity? Who are some creative people you know about? What makes them tick?

WHY MAN CREATES

A SERIES OF EXPLORATIONS, EPISODES AND
COMMENTS ON CREATIVITY
*Note: The film is described in detail to aid re-
call and analysis.*

THE EDIFICE

An edifice is a building, a construction, something which is created. In the conception of the
filmmakers, this animated construction serves
as a metaphor of the civilization that man has
created for himself through history. It is a brisk
sequence, often salted with satire and irony.
Such barbs, however, have an underlying, serious intent: What does it all add up to?

It begins with a group of cavemen discussing
how to kill a huge mammoth. They attempt to
dispatch it with rocks, but are frightened away.
Then they kill it with spears. Already, "progress"
through weapons is implied. The building of the
edifice begins. An ascending construction of
building blocks continues throughout the sequence. Cavemen climb ladders. Quickly the
lever is discovered, then the wheel, hieroglyphics, and fire—a torch is struck with lightning.
The Bronze Age and the Iron Age pass and the
pyramids are built by slaves.

19

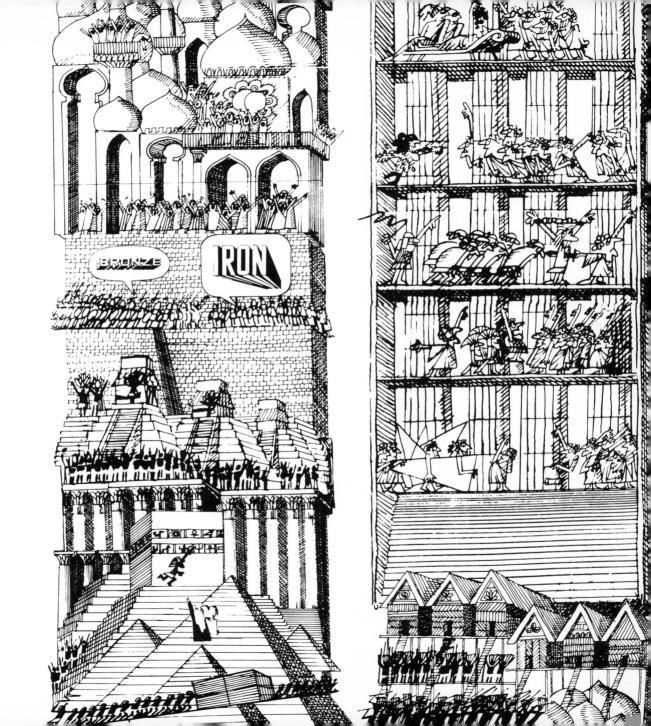

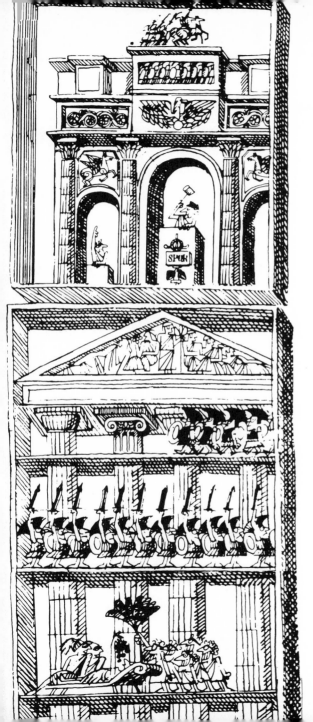

A Greek proclaims "All was in chaos till Euclid rose and made order." This is the first of several philosophical statements in the film. Philosophers ask eternal questions: What is the good life and how do you lead it? Who should rule? The philosopher king? The aristocrat? The people? When one inquisitive slave asks "You mean all the people?" he is furtively stabbed.

The questions continue: What is the nature of the good? What is justice? What is happiness?

The film moves on to Rome, where a tribune proclaims, "Hail, Caesar! Roman law is now in session!"

The walls come tumbling down.

Next come the Dark Ages. In a humorous vignette, a Moslem says, "Allah be praised. I've invented the zero." "What?" asks another. "Nothing, nothing," says the first.

As the film darkens, we see a line of monks and hear them chant, "What is the shape of the earth?" "Flat," is the response. "What happens when you get to the edge?" "You fall off." "Does the earth move?" NEVER.

Then, as we move higher, we hear the assertions: The earth moves, the earth is round, the blood circulates. There are worlds smaller than ours (the invention of the microscope). There are worlds larger than ours (the invention of the telescope).

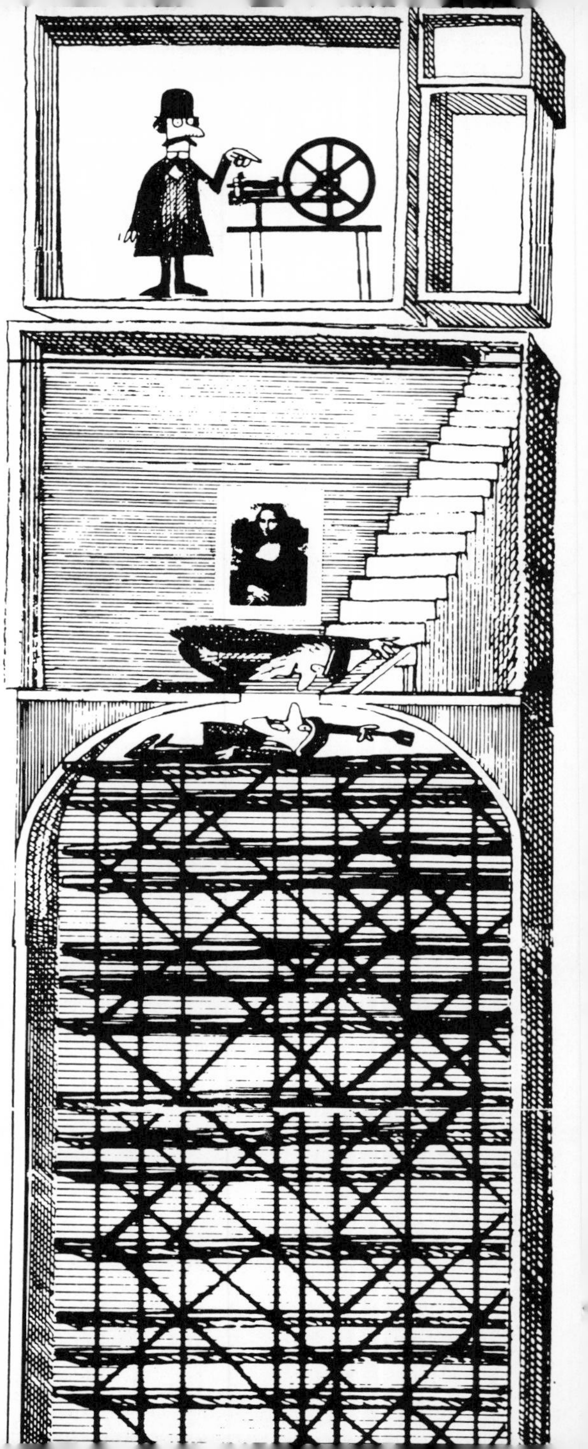

Next, two men are shown painting, one beneath the other.

"Hey, what are you doin'?" asks the top man.

"I'm paintin' the ceiling (Michelangelo). What are you doin'?"

"I'm paintin' the floor," answers the top man. He (Da Vinci) hangs the "Mona Lisa" on the wall then attempts to fly with constructed wings and falls.

The steam engine, the railroad train and the electric light are invented.

Another quick vignette between two men occurs.

"Darwin says man is an animal," says one.

"Rot! Man is not an animal," says the other.

The argument escalates until they fight, very much like animals.

The telegraph is invented.

A man lies on a couch, next to a seated, bearded doctor (Freud). He howls. The doctor says, "Now, shall we start from the beginning."

A germ hops along, saying, "I'm a bug. I'm a germ. I'm a bug. I'm a germ." Spotting a scientist, he says, "Oh, Louis Pasteur!" Reversing his direction, he hops along, saying, "I'm not a bug. I'm not a germ. I'm not a bug."

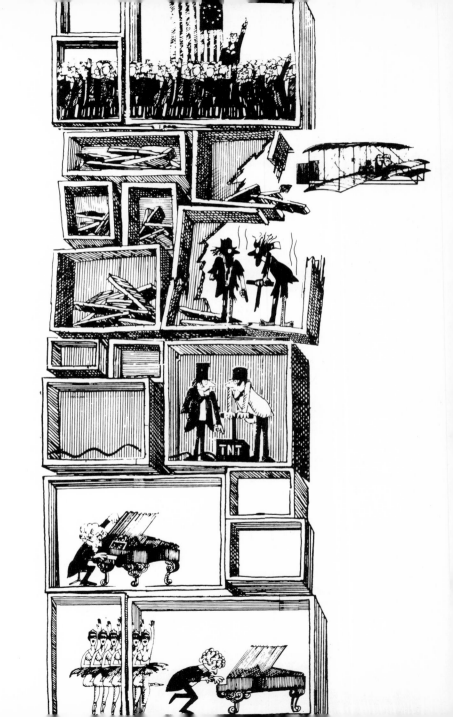

We then see, in quick succession, ballet dancers, then Beethoven, who is yanked off the stage.

Two men stand before a TNT detonator.

"Do you think it'll work, Alfred?" asks one.

"Let's give it a try," Alfred replies.

There is a tremendous explosion.

Covered with dust and debris, the first asks, "What do you think?"

"It worked," says Alfred.

Next, we move quickly through politicians surrounded by people.

We hear:

"All men are created . . . " (Jefferson)

"Life, liberty and the pursuit . . . "

"Government by the people . . . " (Lincoln)

"Workers of the world . . . " (Marx)

"The world must be made safe . . . " (Wilson)

"I see one third of the nation ill-housed . . . " (Roosevelt)

"One World . . . " (Willkie)

Then the invention of the airplane, followed by a tremendous pile of cars. As the camera reaches the top of the heap, it is surrounded by a cloud of pollution. Hovering over the cloud is the symbol of the atom, wavering. We hear a man coughing. Then there is a long, plaintive cry of HELP! On this ironic note, the sequence ends. We are left to ask ourselves, What does it add up to?

The edifice effectively covers the "progress" of mankind with a combination of satire, frequent postholes of philosophical and political vignettes and illustrations of the technological breakthroughs that have shaped today's environment. The sequence is a fast-paced, clever animation that has been brilliantly constructed to make important points about man's contradictory nature, his inventiveness, and the increasing complexity of the world about him as he faces important problems that could destroy the edifice completely.

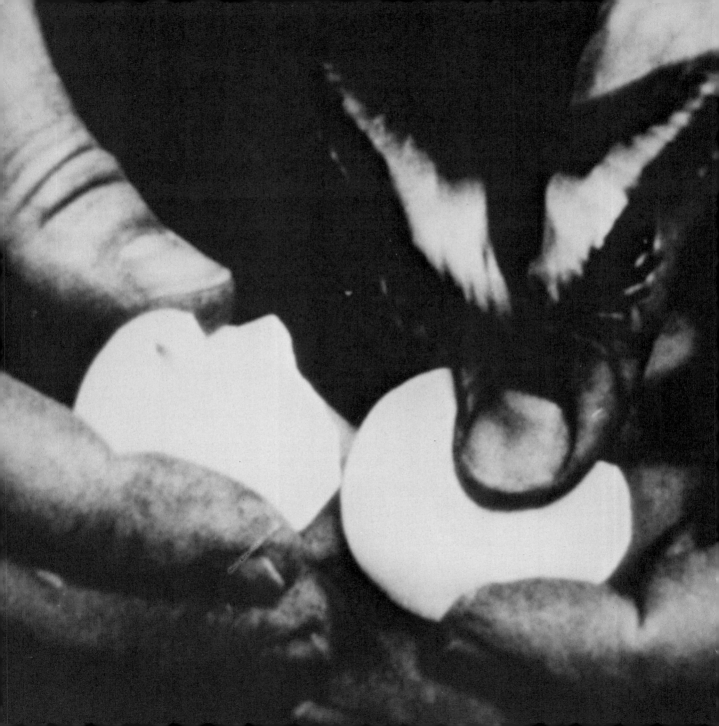

II. FOOLING AROUND: SOMETIMES IDEAS START THAT WAY

This sequence illustrates the role of playfulness in the creative process. The creative person often discovers strange relationships, seemingly weird metaphors. By seeing things differently, he can discover. In short, he manipulates reality in order to discover ideas. Newton, for example, saw the connection between the apple falling and the moon falling, which led him to the theory of gravitation. H.C. Booth saw the possibility of reversing wind, which led to the vacuum cleaner. The Japanese fill plastic bags with water to supplement their dikes, thus fighting water with water.

The sequence begins with a simple, but profound visual metaphor. An egg is cracked and the yolk falls (ordinary experience). Another egg is cracked and thick black liquid emerges (it yields worthless material). Within the third egg, as it opens, is a butterfly (something exquisite and delicate). The metaphor suggests the incubation and creation of an idea. The first egg is ordinary, the second egg produces worthless glop, but sometimes the creative person finds the third egg—the discovery of a splendid idea that lives.

What follows is a series of scenes where far-out special effects clash with ordinary experience to produce satire. A man walks down the street. We hear the words of a scientist discussing the anatomy of the cranium. The divisions of the man's head are illustrated, but they describe the cranium in terms of cuts of meat — filet, pastrami, soup bones, etc. A gentle swipe at scientific jargon?

In a humorous comment on our computer society, a man and a woman face each other in a desk interview. She asks him his zip code, and he replies. Then his Social Security number. Before long, she asks him questions in terms

of numbers, and he replies in numbers. The numbers appear superimposed on the screen with each question and reply until they blot out the entire scene in darkness.

A crowd of people wait to cross the street. The sign flashes "WALK." When the crowd reaches the middle, it flashes "STOP." "TURN." "READY." They proceed to do calisthenics to the directions of the stop sign—ONE, TWO, ONE, TWO.

Next, we see a dancer doing a dance similar to the twist. Her head thrashes wildly. The frame freezes, a hand opens up the lid on her head, drops in two scoops of ice cream and some milk, then closes it. Her head continues to shake.

A hippie speaks, suggesting that the important thing is to break out—that freedom is the important thing. A hand opens up the lid on his head and pulls out a sign reading "MOTHER."

A middle-aged society matron sips a martini and chatters about how she knows things have changed, but things are constant . . . that the younger generation merely wants to satisfy their own egos . . . The hand opens up the lid on her head, a face appears and yells into the hole, "HELLO, DOWN THERE!" The echo amplifies her vacuous chatter.

All three of the lid vignettes are vivid visual examples of how the creative person might see fresh connections in common experiences. They are visual puns that comment on conforming, frivolous youth, the conforming non-conformist, and the tendentious conformity of an older generation that tends to think in bromides.

The sequence becomes serious as we watch a child swinging, superimposed over a crowd on the street. The words we hear are: "Where do ideas come from? From looking at one thing and seeing another. From fooling around, play-

ing with possibilities, changing, speculating, pushing, pulling, transforming. If you're lucky, you come up with something maybe worth saving, using, and building on. That's where the game stops and the work begins."

As we hear the narration, we see a shot of a child swinging, dandelion pollen released from the stem into the air, the face of a girl against a screen, superimposed over the crowd, and the grace of a bird in flight.

The statement at the end neatly sums up how the creative person thinks, illustrating it poetically in both visual and verbal terms.

III. THE PROCESS

This is a section which shows the eccentric artist attempting to create an unusual sculpture using large light geometric forms. As he tries and fails, we see stills of Edison that move gradually from age to youth. We hear Edison's words: "I admitted that I had days of such discouragement that I ached to give it up. I guess what kept me going was faith—the kind you have when you're young and don't know any better."

The artist works at his structure again, but it falls about him. We see stills of Hemingway, moving again from age to youth, as we hear: "When the stuff comes alive and turns crazy on you, a writer had better be in pretty good shape, with good legs, and a counter-punch, and ready to fight like hell to the bloody end."

rying once more, the artist sees another tentative structure collapse, but this time his hand punches through one of the blocks, triggering an idea. We see a still of Einstein and hear his words: "As one grows older, one sees the impossibility of imposing one's will on the chaos with brute force. But if you're patient, there may come that moment, when while eating an apple, the solution presents itself politely and says, 'Here I am'."

The solution has presented itself to the artist. Using the hands, heads and other parts of model dummies he creates a bizarre mechanical sculpture that moves in martial rhythm. Calling his wife Marge he shows her his pride and joy. Marge suggests that all it needs is an American flag (a juxtaposition of the familiar with the strange, the cliché with the fresh approach).

V. THE JUDGMENT

Here, we see a crowd of people evaluating the artist's creation. There is a variety of comments, most of them brutally negative. "What a piece of garbage that is."

"Sick!"

"It's degrading."

"It'll never fly, Orville."

"It represents the decline of the West."

"That's where the taxpayers' money goes."

The artist, dressed in a cowboy suit, defends his work. In this surrealistic sequence, he shoots members of the crowd and is shot in return. Full of lead, he falls in slow motion, then hears words that suggest hope. A woman's voice says, "I don't know. I like it." As his face lights up, he hears her say, "The material alone must be worth at least $100." He falls, squelched, shot down by the crowd.

The sequence symbolizes the labor and vision that goes into the creative act, and the all-too-frequent resistance of the public to the work of the creative artist. The symbolic artist of the sequence is destroyed by the public. Yet those who succeed have the courage to persist. Edison, Hemingway, and Einstein continued to work in the face of adversity, believing in their visions. It is worth noting that Alexander Graham Bell was turned down when he first tried to sell the telephone because "there was no need for it," that Pasteur was ostracized by the scientists of his day, that Edison was scoffed at by contemporary experts who felt that his idea of the electric light was unworthy of attention, and that the inventor of the Xerox copying process took four years to find a backer after he had invented it. The annals of history are full of the stories of artists like Van Gogh, Modigliani, Edgar Allan Poe, and Cervantes who persisted against adversity that would have defeated ordinary men.

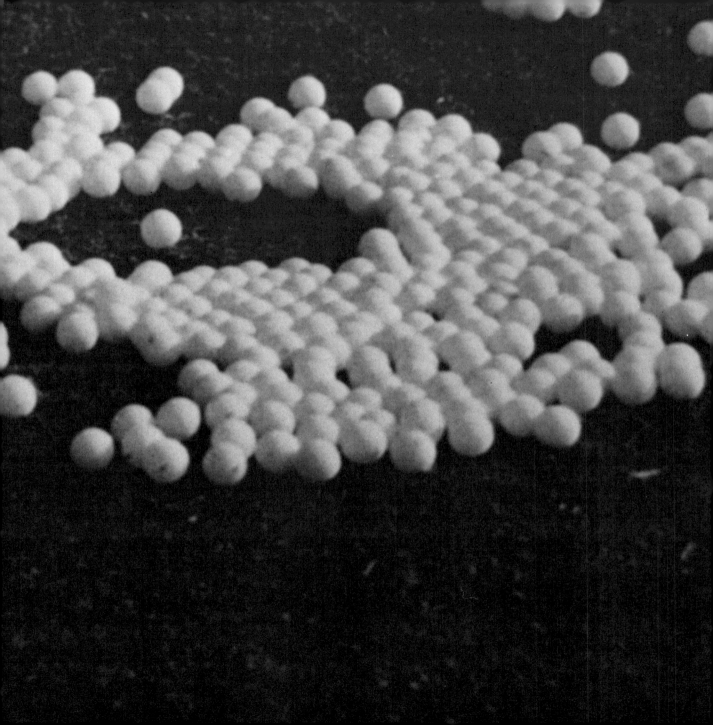

V. A PARABLE

This sections opens with shots of Ping-Pong balls moving along an assembly line. One of the balls is obviously different from the others. A special selector isolates it and rejects it by throwing it down a chute, where it misses the trash can and lands on the sidewalk. It is confused at first, then discovers that it has considerable bounce. It proceeds to bounce along, over cars in the street, until it comes to a beautiful park. Many normal balls congregate to watch it bounce. The odd ball performs, bouncing higher and higher until on the final bounce, it does not return to earth. The viewer then sees these words appear on the screen:

THERE ARE SOME WHO SAY HE IS COMING BACK AND WE HAVE ONLY TO WAIT.

THERE ARE SOME WHO SAY HE BURST UP THERE BECAUSE BALL WAS NOT MEANT TO FLY.

AND THERE ARE SOME WHO MAINTAIN THAT HE LANDED SAFELY IN A PLACE WHERE BALLS BOUNCE HIGH.

The final words indicate the variety of response to any kind of mystery, whether it be creative performance, or an unexplained phenomenon. The words are echoes of public responses of the past that include faith, skepticism, and sentimentality.

VI. A DIGRESSION

An animated sequence shows two snails conversing. The first says:

"Have you ever thought that radical ideas threaten institutions, then become institutions, and in turn reject radical ideas that threaten institutions?"

"No," replies the other snail.

"Gee, for a minute I thought I had something," says the first snail.

If the creative thinker's sensitivity yields to conservative rejection by his peers, his freedom to think and create will be constricted. The artist continues to probe his environment, to play with associations, and to create in spite of outward resistance and derision.

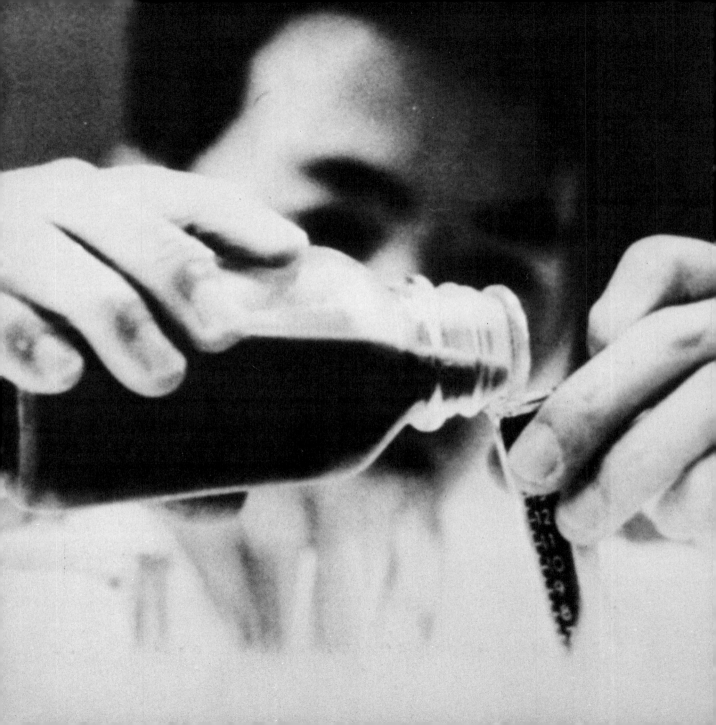

VII. THE SEARCH: WORK IN PROGRESS ON NEW IDEAS

Four research scientists are interviewed about their project. The first has been working on a cure for cancer for 20 years. He feels that he has been making progress, and that there will possibly be an answer to how a normal cell changes into a cancer cell in five years.

The second scientist has been working on the world food problem. In spite of progress, the problem has expanded as discoveries have occurred. Due to the population increase, two out of three people in the world go to bed hungry every night. He has developed tomatoes and peas that can grow in places where they have never been able to flourish before. He has also developed cereals with the nutritive value of meat. He feels that the problem may be under control in 15 or 20 years.

The third scientist has been working for many years on the theory of the origin of the universe. It presently appears that an absence of helium on distant stars may disprove the "Big Bang" theory, but again, what he sees in telescopes may not be true.

The fourth scientist has been working on a problem for seven years, and now finds that he was on the wrong track. Asked what he will do next, he says, "I don't know."

The section effectively shows the long-term commitment and energy that goes into scientific, creative research. It also shows the possibility of failure after much effort. Creative scientists live with the possibility of years of their lives spent on ultimate failure, yet they persist.

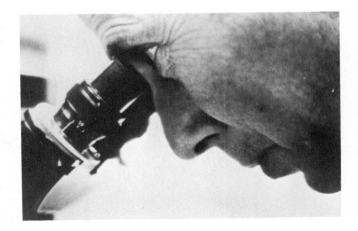

VIII. THE MARK

This section is not labelled, but it is a celebration and summation of the creative process. Showing the art of the ancients, monuments, great paintings, writings, and scientific inventions leading up to the present, we hear the following narration as creativity passes in review:

"Why does man create? Men have struggled against time, against decay, against destruction, against death. Some have cried out in torment and in agony. Some have fought with arrogance and fierce pride. Some challenged the gods, matching power with power (shot of rocket).

Some have celebrated life. Some have burned with faith. Some have spoken in voices we no longer understand. Some have spoken eloquently (shots of work by Degas, Rembrandt, Mark Twain, Handel, Thomas Jefferson).

Some have spoken inarticulately, some haltingly. Some have been almost mute (shots of grafitti on walls, including 'LOVE WHO?' 'BOO', 'I AM').

Yet among all the variety of human expression, a thread of connection, a common mark, can be seen. That urge to look into oneself and out at the world and say, 'This is what I am. I am unique. I am here. I am'."

The film ends with a shot of a young boy on the beach, running toward the sea, as birds soar skyward. The dignity and potential of the individual to create is the serious, inspirational note on which the film concludes.

REACTIONS OF STUDENTS WHO SAW THE FILM:

The following reactions were spontaneous writings selected from two groups of students who saw *Why Man Creates* in California and Virginia. Their ages range from 15 to 18.

"It made me realize all the things in the world that I would like to do and it gave me the feeling that I could paint like Renoir or write like Hemingway if I really put my mind to it."

"The movie made a sort of wonderful, joyful tingle run all up and down within me. It made me feel like maybe in this world we live there are people who can create rather than destruct, that in this world there is a place where one can just be oneself."

"I feel like a person and that I should do my thing. It made me feel like someone."

It makes me want to delve into my mind and really feel and look for the real me. With this film in mind, the question that is posed to me is, 'Do I have any creative ability and can I be the real me?' Excellent."

"I feel like wow! The world has been creating for billions of years and here I am! Even though all these people (scientists, artists, etc.) have taken decades to devote themselves to looking for ideas and even though they haven't come up with a solution they are still looking!"

'It made me feel odd; it presented questions that I have always tried to answer—it was so indirect it made me think in an abstract manner."

"The movie makes me feel that there are still some people who dare to be different. They dare to create something rather than just taking an old thing and trying to make it new. It made me want to create something unique. It moved me in such a way that I say Bravo! to the creators of this film. I say this very strongly . . ."

'This made me feel happy and proud to be living. It showed me man can do so many things with himself. It inspired me to try to look to my own creativity and see what I can do. It also made me feel like an individual unlike anyone else and made me realize everyone is different in their creative ways."

'Started out sad and depressing because it satirized us—our society and civilization. But then it gets you to laugh—probably at yourself. It's very deep with meaning and intonation—tries successfully to make you stop and think of life and yourself. Ending is beautiful."

'Fantastic! Beautifully done. It says in scenes, pictures, and suggestions what I've never been able to put into words. A beautiful creation with more meaning than any film I have ever seen."

"I felt confused. Not confused because I didn't understand the premise behind the movie, but because I have many ideas in my head and I have not as yet learned how to express them creatively. This movie taught me how to look at commonplace objects in new ways."

"What we need are things to make us think, not in little squares and cubes but in an uninhibited manner. What this film did was to make me think. This film did not simply present a question and then answer it. It left this to the viewer. It made me ask myself, 'What is the meaning?'"

45

Most of the comments were in this positive vein, but there were a few negative ones, which shows that no matter how great a film may be, some people won't like it.

"Nothing!"

"Puzzled."

"The movie stinks. Horribly!"

"I fell asleep during the last 3/4's of the film!"

AFTER THE FILM:

1. Describe an experience where you have attempted to create something. Share the problems and processes of your creative attempt.
2. Find two completely unrelated objects and see if you can create a connection between them that makes them an interesting "work of art."
3. Write about the constructive and destructive results of some of the great inventions or creations of the past.
4. Create a collage or an unusual environment which represents your perception of the present world. Use sound, smell and touch, as well as visual stimuli.
5. Research the life of a creative person and attempt to show the problems he had to overcome and how he was able to achieve results.
6. What about yourself? In what ways do you have the potential to be creative?
7. Interview a professional artist, writer, filmmaker, actor, or musician. Attempt, through your interview, to discover his methods of working and the roots of his creative process.
8. Interview an ordinary person. Attempt, through your interview, to determine in what ways he or she is creative. This might be through a job, a hobby, or another area.

9. Find examples of creative photography, music, literature, sculpture, or other art. Why, do you feel, are these outstanding examples of creativity?
10. You might examine your town or city. Can you find unusual examples of creativity in architecture, advertising, window displays, or any other field?
11. Watch television for two evenings. Take notes on examples of creativity on the tube.
12. What is the best movie you have seen in the past year? What creative elements make it an excellent work of art?

"It would seem apparent that there is no *one* creative process, and there may well be as many creative processes as there are creative people."

—H. Herbert Fox, *"A Critique on Creativity in the Sciences"*

"Creativity is the ability to *see* (or be aware) and to *respond.*"

—Eric Fromm, *"The Creative Attitude"*

"Creativity is the encounter of the intensively conscious human being with his world."

—Rollo May, *"The Nature of Creativity"*

WHY MAN CREATES

SOHN: Mr. Bass, what is *Why Man Creates* saying to the audience? If it is possible to put it in verbal terms, why did you make it?

SAUL BASS: I was trying to demonstrate in both the content and form of the film the nature of the creative process. And, in passing, to celebrate the variety, the richness and importance of the creative vision. The intent of the film is to give those who look at it, and who are probably not working (as a life-commitment) in creative areas, a sense of what it *feels* like to work creatively . . . the agony, the frustration, the discipline, the pleasure, the messiness, the orderliness, the failure, (and in the case of the scientists) the aberrant nature of time when you are engaged in the process.

I tried to communicate what this life-commitment feels like, because it is an area that has been confused by shoddy writing, bad movies, and loose talk.

I wanted the persons looking at it to make their own judgments about themselves and their experiences—to have something to compare them with, so that their frustrations won't necessarily be seen as failures, reflecting their own inabilities, but be perceived within the context of the nature of the creative process. Failure is characteristic of this process. A young creative person often thinks that he is inadequate because it is difficult to solve the problem. He thinks that this is a weakness. But you eventually find out that everybody struggles. There is no shortcut.

I would like the young people who see this film to be able to equate their own failures, their own difficulties, their own enjoyment, their own messes, with what the film says.

In the film, I deal with the shakers . . . the great creative shakers of the world. Some people may feel that the film implies that creativity is a property of only those who make the great revolutions. I did not intend it to do so, but the issues are most clearly understood when seen in terms of this group.

SOHN: If we can talk about how you made the film, I think *The Edifice* sequence, which begins the picture, is one of the most splendid pieces of animation I have seen. It is humorous, yet it is highly instructive. What did you intend there?

BASS: I think what we wanted to do in the edifice was to show the variety, the richness, the multiplicity of creative acts in building what we call civilization. Civilization, in its most positive terms, is the accumulation of creative insights in terms of painting, sculpture, philosophy, poetry, and various other forms that interpret the human condition . . . man's view of himself and his world.

It also includes the revolutionary scientific breakthroughs in understanding the nature of the world in which he exists. But investigating these things is not always positive. Sometimes creativity results in something that can be destructive. This is symbolized by the allusion to TNT—Alfred Nobel's invention. We know that he spent the rest of his life atoning for the destructiveness of his invention.

We see the Roman Empire collapsing around the creation of law, the juxtaposition of the positive and negative. We've come to think of Rome as a weak echo of Greek society, with corruption and decadence added. Actually, this was true, but Rome also made important contributions to the world.

SOHN: What were some of the problems you faced in designing this section?

BASS: The great difficulty in the edifice was how to sum up an age in a few seconds. The form of each section of the edifice was precisely designed to reflect the spirit of that age. For instance, the whole Greek period, which runs 20 seconds, is intended to reflect the contribution of the Greek culture to history—namely, its discursive and investigatory character. Its form in the edifice acquired the particular character of a series of discussions, and an attempt to reveal some of the contradictions of this period. In spite of the fact that it dealt with the expansion of the human psyche and intellect, it still was a slave society, built upon slavery. When one character asks, "Who shall rule the State?" one voice asserts "The aristocrat," another "the philosopher-king," a chorus "the people." But when the slave says, "You mean *all* of the people?" he gets it right through the gut with a sword as one of the Greeks continues, "What is the nature of justice?" never seeing, as Greek society never perceived, this essential inner contradiction.

On the other hand, the whole Middle Ages, the "Dark Ages," was approached from another point of view. We conceived it as a kind of mystic, dark section with a Gregorian chant which posed a number of questions—for which the chant gave the wrong answers—naturally.

The Renaissance as the age of enlightenment is expressed by having everything light up again. There is the breakthrough concept, opening the doors to knowledge. The windows and doors open, but there is the oppresive hand of the church, the prevalent religious orders which felt threatened by these empirical, scientific developments. We symbolize that by a black hand coming in and always closing the door. It is a fight between men of reason, the creative figures who open the doors, and the repressive forces of the day, reacting by closing the doors.

SOHN: Were there any ideas that you had to leave out?

BASS: We lost a lot of ideas which we simply didn't have time for. In the Renaissance, there were many other doors we omitted.

With the writing sequence, where we had a man going around the block, hacking out hieroglyphics like a typewriter would—tickety, tickety, bing! tickety, tickety, bing!—we originally also had a couple of bystanders there. The one says, "Hey, this is called writing!" The other says, "It'll never replace yelling!"

Part of the concept of the edifice was to develop a feeling of tremendous richness. Even though we spanned thousands of years of time, it was intended to feel like a fantastic pell-mell of achievement going by.

SOHN: Why did you choose to animate that sequence?

BASS: Well, animation seemed the way to do it because I felt it would be the most convincing technique for what we wanted to say.

SOHN: What did you intend in the next sequence the *Fooling Around* section?

BASS: The purpose of that sequence was to show how the creative process begins, how it grows out of the intrinsic character of the creative personality. What makes the creative person different? I think it is the capacity to manipulate reality without inhibitions, to manipulate the environment, and to use observation as a base for imagination.

attempted to show a reality situation and what happens when a creative personality looks at reality and says "What if?" What if we stood it on its head? What if we stood *ourselves* on our head? What if we did it backwards? What if we did the last thing first and the first thing last? It is what we call the "fooling around attitude" that makes you feel free to try anything without fear of being foolish.

The ability to fantasize without getting "uptight" is important, to fantasize without becoming concerned or anxious . . . to freely leap from one associative concept to another, and jump without a premeditated plan. You allow the accident to occur, the subsconscious to emerge. You allow a strange positioning of elements that you would never usually allow, rationally or logically. You observe something interesting and allow it in turn to catapult you further.

The "fooling around attitude" may not result in a solution, but it is the process through which you begin to develop the elements that may lead to one.

We must be very careful to differentiate between "fooling around" and the serious creative process . . . which is not "fun." It is hard work and agony, as well as joy. But "fooling around" is the beginning.

We used several examples to try to describe the process of altering reality, playing with it. Eggs are eggs, but if you stop to think about it, what if eggs contain grease, or ugly things? Or, what if they contain something beautiful, like a butterfly? What does it mean? Thinking like that is just fooling around. Maybe it will lead to something.

What is significant about the head opening sequence and people-doing-calisthenics-in-the-street sequences and the number sequence is that these are all reality situations which are then manipulated by a creative observer. In the number sequence, it starts with the secretary asking for the man's Social Security number and eventually they end up talking in numbers. Reality is altered. The meaning of that manipulation? That's open, obviously. You can say, yes, we are living in a number society, we are no longer communicating in human terms—we communicate in ciphers. Or we can say that all languages are arbitrary components, and numbers are no different, as a language, than letters or words. There is no reason why language could not have developed in terms of numbers as easily as it did in terms of letters. There are all kinds of positive, negative, neutral, and speculative connotations to what the meaning of the sequence is.

The whole sequence operates on two levels. One is process. It says start with reality. Manipulate. Change. The second level is meaning—what does the manipulation mean? That's another matter.

SOHN: The next section is where the hard work takes place, then—the *Process* section?

BASS: Yes. The artist has constructed his "thing." He thinks it's great. His long-suffering wife is a little more dubious. He then submits it to society, and these people represent the reaction of society to his creation. Society's reaction runs the gamut from that of faint puzzlement to true irritation, anger and violent hostility. He reacts. He defends his work. It is not only his bruised ego, but also his belief in what he has done that causes him to defend his work as vigorously as he does.

It was very interesting that after we shot that sequence, the Chicago Picasso events occured. This was one of those things—art precedes life.

51

I was very fascinated when I read the papers as to how closely we had predicted the reaction of the crowd in Chicago.

SOHN: With the process and society reacting sequences, were there any problems that plagued you?

BASS: There was one thing that was difficult to cover in that sequence which is, I think, an important idea. You see an artist, a creative person, can accept criticism or can live with criticism much more easily than with being ignored. Criticism makes you feel alive. If somebody is bothered enough by what you have done to speak vituperatively about it, you feel you have touched a nerve and you are at least "in touch." You are not happy that he doesn't like it, but you feel you are in contact with life.

But when it moves no one enough, one way or the other, to react to it—that is when you truly reject the artist. Indifference is the most serious and the most difficult thing for artists to live with.

SOHN: How did you get those fantastic reactions from people?

BASS: The sequence was shot in downtown Los Angeles at Broadway and 7th. We had a small group of people that I assembled who understood the sequence and knew what we were after. We set ourselves up as a camera crew— a TV crew. We tried to create a condition which would attract passers-by to the crowd. I had about 15 people who were arguing, gathered around me. I was the interviewer. People stopped and were curious. When they did, we would get them up front and ask them certain questions. We presented provocative issues. I had an architectural drawing of a proposed toll booth on the freeway, ostensibly to raise additional taxes. Each time, I explained, one leaves the freeway, you would have to pay 50 cents. Our question was, "What do you think of that, sir?" Well, that got a pretty good reaction.

Then, we had another one—a very, very strong Picasso. It is a dismembered figure—the arms and legs and head kind of float. This is the one where the black man reacted, "It seems to me that it is some kind of servile mechanism in man's mind." We got other reactions to it. It was introduced as the latest acquisition of the County Museum. I mentioned some outlandish price, and that's when the guy yelled. "That's the taxpayers' money! That's what they are doing with the taxpayers' money!"

Then I had a third provocation. We painted a nude girl psychedelically. Using enlarged photographs I introduced this as a new fashion development—the new summer clothes—the "no-clothes" clothes. Paint it on in the morning and wash it off at night. What do you think of that? Well, *that* got some interesting reactions.

Between these various devices, we were able to simulate reactions that we could use as though the crowd was reacting to what the young man had built.

A few reactions were staged, you understand. Some of them were written in, but some of these things you could never stage, like that Nebraska woman. That kind of word construction you would never dream of writing. You never write, "I'm an old, old American, and you know how they feel, from Nebraska." Just too good. You would never figure out how to get that kind of authentic wrongness into the thing.

SOHN: How long did it take to shoot?

BASS: Three days, spread over a period of time.

53

SOHN: I'm very curious about that delightful *Parable* section. What was your intention there?

BASS: It was a kind of summary of what we had said before, in another form.

SOHN: It parallels the experience of the artist, then?

BASS: Yes. The ball is rejected and separated from his peers and his society. Society views the ball as a freak and ejects him into the world, outside the pall. On a more positive note, as he wanders around unhappy, he decides that "he is what he is." If he is a high bouncer, he is a high bouncer. Apparently high bouncers are repugnant, looked upon with disdain. But what can he do? He happens to bounce high, he is what he is, and that's what he is going to do. He is going to go through life "doing his thing." As he bounces through life, he finds a certain exultation in his bouncing. He learns to like it. He loves what he is. He believes in his own integrity, the value of what he is to himself. He experiences self-fulfillment and realizes, more and more, his potential for high bouncing.

SOHN: And society reacts.

BASS: Society, in a funny kind of way, notes this unusual quality. It not only notes that the ball is different, but also, in a deep intuitive way, not fully understanding it, kind of admires it. They think, "He is a pretty high bouncer. That's kind of wild. I don't know that I would want to do that, but high bouncing is something to watch." His disappearance into the blue stirs up the whole ball population and raises a lot of speculative thinking. "What does it mean?" they ask. Some say "He's coming back and we have only to wait"; others "He burst up there because . . . "; and maybe "He landed safely in a place where balls bounce high."

SOHN: How did you design and animate that section?

BASS: The impression is that you are looking at the same ball all through the sequence, but you aren't. We used all kinds of balls—Ping Pong balls, super balls, beach balls, and tennis balls, depending on what we were doing. When we were bouncing through traffic, for example, we had to use a large ball because a normal ball could not be seen at that distance. The small white ball blended into the environment, so we used a big beach ball. That was not animated. We threw the ball until it bounced right. We did that on a Sunday morning in the street downtown, where there was no traffic. We blocked off the street and had 65 people there—staff, friends, and relatives. They all brought their cars, and we kept them coming through.

SOHN: Did you use "stop-action" animation at all?

BASS: No. Animating it was complicated. Some of it was just rolling the balls and blowing air at the balls. Some of it was shot in reverse. The balls were not coming together—they were breaking apart.

SOHN: What do you feel you developed in *The Search* section?

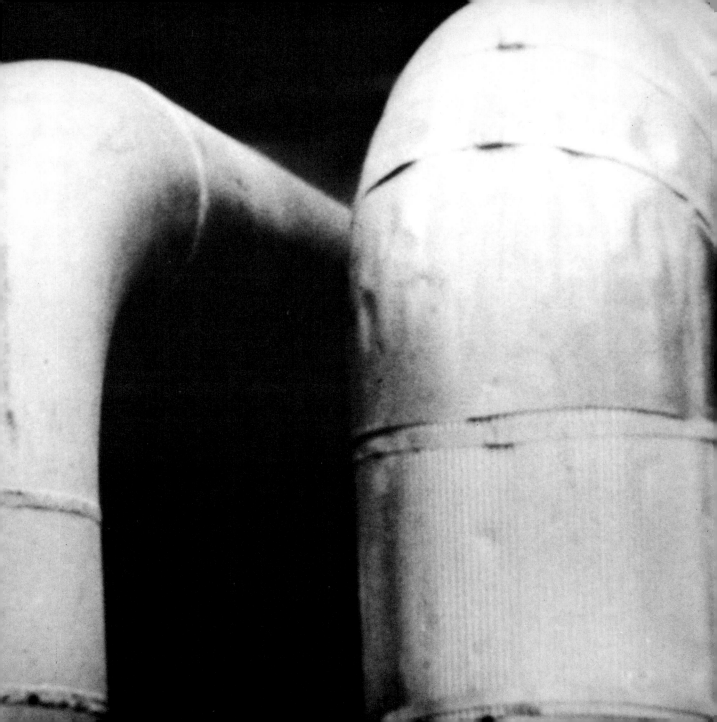

BASS: I was interested in projecting a unique trait of the creative personality. The whole "time syndrome" is completely different in creative people. I carefully built each sequence to lead us to see how each researcher was spending a fantastic amount of time on what he was doing. And each one knows he might fail. Greenstein, one of the major contributors to the Big Bang theory, possibly, invalidates the whole theory by a recent discovery. He does it to himself. He says, "If this apparent discovery is true, the Big Bang theory is false, and we will have to develop an entirely new theory to account for the origin of the universe."

Then Bonner, working on world population says, "since we started working on this problem, the problem has doubled. Two out of three people are going hungry, instead of one out of three." But he is optimistic.

SOHN: There does seem to be an aura of tenacious optimism reflected by these men.

BASS: Everybody is very optimistic. They are not discouraged because they are so absorbed with the fascination of the process. Dr. Bonner cheerfully says, "Oh, we'll get the whole thing under control in 15 or 20 years."

When I interviewed Dr. Dulbecco he said, "Now we know enough about the problem, so that we can now make a conclusive experiment." One would think that he was a month or so away from the goal . . . and he continues, "We are very optimistic . . . and we hope to have positive results in, say, five years." Marvelous!

SOHN: Then you wanted to illustrate that time means very little to the involved, creative personality?

BASS: Yes, and this quality is very exciting. Some of these people will work and spend their whole lifetimes, happy, to think that they may be able to uncover a corner of what they are working on, let alone solve the whole problem. It only takes a few years to build the biggest oil cracking plant. It only took ten years to build the Aswan Dam. But that's nothing. These guys are talking in terms of lifetimes. And the poor fellow at the end, who after seven years of work "has hit a blank wall." He will go on.

SOHN: How would you summarize your intent in this sequence?

BASS: It has a double intent. One is to demonstrate that time is irrelevant to creative people whether scientists or artists. A painter spends his whole life solving a problem on the canvas.

Another thing I wanted to say is that this is, indeed, a strange activity. I wanted to say, "Indeed, if this is so frustrating, so seemingly hopeless, so difficult, why does man engage in this activity?" I wanted to give myself the platform from which to launch into that final discussion of the basic human origins of creativity.

57

SOHN: The film begins in a light vein, then seems to become more serious as it draws to a close.

BASS: It does move from a lighter beginning to a more serious conclusion. But even in the humorous parts, there is a serious intent. I very much like the kind of humor that freezes on your lips. Where, halfway through the laugh, you wonder what you are laughing at. That is "learning" humor, as well as "feeling" humor. I wanted the whole film to begin with a "laugh it up" feeling, then suddenly it isn't funny any more.

SOHN: Then you think that humor is an excellent device for educating?

BASS: I believe very deeply in the value of humor. Somehow, you learn more when you are laughing—when you can sense the good feeling and warm intent of the person who is talking to you. You are more open to positive and joyful people, even if you don't agree with what they have to say.

SOHN: What do you mean by "humor"?

BASS: When I say humor, I use the word very broadly. It can be wit, or personal warmth. It can be friendliness, combined with a sense of seeing some of the irony, the contrasts, and the juxtapositions of life in relation to the material you are dealing with. I believe very strongly in the value of humor and the beautiful as avenues for reaching people and helping them to open their minds to what is said.

SOHN: Do you feel you come to any conclusions in this film?

BASS: This is an open-ended film. I don't come to any conclusions, although naturally one can't be neutral on any subject. One always has a point of view. I think it would have been presumptuous of me to have come to a conclusion in any event. I was being completely honest in the film. I don't know what all the answers are. For instance, I do not take the position that society is wrong in its hostility to a new idea. I would have to say that it is often correct for society to resist new ideas. Most new ideas are wrong, and some are even dangerous. Therefore it is appropriate for society to set up a mesh or sieve that filters new ideas. Our real attention should focus on the dimension of the holes in that sieve.

SOHN: So many young people react with great enthusiasm to *Why Man Creates*. Many times, however, they have difficulty with articulating just what it is that moves them.

BASS: Apparently students do feel stirred by the film and I think they are stirred (without necessarily being able to express it) by two basic ideas that form the conclusion of the film . . . the origins of the creative act. We say that the creative act has to be understood as having its sources in two urges which exist simultaneously or individually. Man creates to leave his mark on his time, as a denial of mortality, to say "Look at me . . . I was here . . ." He also creates out of a need to identify himself, to himself . . . to say, as we say at the end of the film, "I am unique . . . I am here . . . I am."

"The curious world which we inhabit is more wonderful than it is convenient, more beautiful than it is useful; it is more to be admired than it is to be used."

—Henry David Thoreau

"Both Wordsworth and Thoreau knew that when the light of common day seemed no more than common, it was because of something lacking within them, not because of something lacking in it, and what they asked for was eyes to see a universe they knew was worth seeing."

—Joseph Wood Krutch

"Perhaps if we were franker on personal creativity, we might reach out and occasionally touch, with a passing radiance, some other star in the night."

—Loren Eiseley, *The Mind as Nature*
© 1962, Harper & Row, Publishers, Inc.

60

II. THE PRECISE EYE: A Sharper Vision

LEAF
DUNES
WATERS OF YOSEMITE
AUTUMN: FROST COUNTRY

All the films in this unit were shot and edited by Fred Hudson, a filmmaker gifted with sensitive, poetic and precise eyes. His emphasis is the world of nature and wilderness. About his work, he has said: "I make films in the way I do because I feel there is something *out there* that is worth knowing about, that is worth seeing, that is worth interpreting. Film would be a tool for sharpening my focus.

The natural world is an inspiring place. I try with motion picture photography to find that which is pure poetry, and to implant those images on film. I am not trying to say we should save our forests and animals so much as to say: here before us are poems, and there are endless poems. Let's look at them. Film is a record of poetry. It is a treatment of something that is already there."

That Fred Hudson succeeds admirably is obvious from experiencing these films. Like Wordsworth, Thoreau, and Robert Frost, Fred Hudson has the intensity of perception and the standards of perfection that result in the vivid, poetic experience. What great poets do with words, Fred does with images. If we study these films carefully, we will learn much about observation and relationships. So much writing and conversation is riddled with clichés, vague amorphous thoughts—in short, with hot air. To create verbal images, one much hone thoughts and shape them with precise details that enable the reader or listener to perceive and imagine with sharp clarity. The communicator must labor and distill to induce not only sight, but insight. It is no simple task, but it is one that we should all work toward incessantly. "Easy writing makes hard reading," as one great writer said. This statement applies to all forms of communication.

As we work with these films, we will encounter precision shaped into art. There will be ample opportunity to concentrate on this aspect of observation and interpretation. These films merit careful study and discussion as models of what the precise eye can achieve. Perhaps you will want to follow up with writing and other creative activities that build upon the theme of the films.

61

LEAF

A film produced by David Adams.
Filmed and edited by Fred Hudson.

Time: 7 min.; Color

Distributed by Pyramid

A leaf swirls to the ground.
A butterfly floats through the air.
Oh, time—where do you go?
—Julie Cutler, Grade 8

The experience of *Leaf* is deceptively simple. It is easy to miss the elements of design in the film, such as the rhythm, flow, and variety of the editing, the varying lengths of the shots both in terms of space and time, and the subtle inclusion of aspects of the environment that set the scene and the different moods of the picture. To screen it several times, is to gain a deeper appreciation of the art and craft of the film. The musical sound track by Fred Katz gives sensitive support to the visual experience, accenting the different moods and tonal qualities. The music was composed after the film was made, and it reveals an extraordinary skill of auditory interpretation.

THE FILM:

Leaf begins with a close-up of a yellow leaf dangling from a limb, against the background of mountains in Yosemite. The camera cuts to close-ups of flower pods, reeds and a clump of grass in the stream. The camera catches the leaves of another tree in the radiance of autumn. Glimmering water is glimpsed through the reeds along the lake. Then there is a shot of deer grazing. Suddenly something catches their attention. It appears to be the rustle of a breeze coming up. Pan shots of rustling leaves and blowing boughs reveal the rising wind. So do the clouds moving in the sky. The deer dash off. The grass blows more wildly; the leaf separates from the tree. The film cuts to a shot of a blue jay, ap-

pearing to look at the leaf. The leaf drifts across a rock and into the air. It wavers, teetering and tottering in the wind, moving upward with the air currents, then floating downward. It touches the side of the mountain and a shot from below shows it floating downward to a rock. The leaf dances along the rock, then skitters across it and is airborne again as we see a fuller view of the surrounding beauty of the mountains.

The leaf waltzes to the music as it continues its descent. Finally it settles on a stream. It floats slowly along the water, between narrow rocks, then swirls as the current grows stronger. It moves more rapidly. A striking circular pan shot looks upward at the leaves on a tree. The leaf floats beneath a small log bridge, into the darker shadows. There is a shot through branches that follows it into more intense shadows. The film ends as the leaf disappears into total darkness, and the cycle is completed.

AFTER THE FILM:

Leaf is one of the best examples available to illustrate the extended visual metaphor. It may elicit a variety of responses, but many people see it as a representation of a life span, a natural cycle that symbolizes much of human experience. The film's lyrical simplicity is a conception that is at the other end of the spectrum

rom the fast-cutting visual gallop of many mod-
rn filmmakers. It's a good idea to see the film
nore than once, especially if you want to study
Judson's precise camera technique and expert
diting.

1. Write about the leaf's experience in another
   form of poetry.
2. Could you write a narrative story based on
   Leaf? It might be from the point-of-view of
   the leaf, or from one of the animals seeing
   the leaf.
3. How is the leaf like a metaphor? A simile?
   An allegory? A parable? A symbol? Where
   is the climax in the narrative? The denoue-
   ment? How many moods are there in the
   film? Describe them. What are the rhythms
   in the film, combined with the music?
4. Compare the parable of the leaf to the parable of the Ping-Pong ball in *Why Man Creates.* Include other parables you know about.
   Discuss or write about them.
5. Write a story about another object such as
   a tree, a paperclip, a hat, a house, a bird,
   a statue, a garbage can, or a church.
6. In your observer's notebook, describe things
   that change or go through cycles.
7. Some poems you might like to read are e.e.
   cummings' "1 (leaf falls)," and "A Wind Has
   Blown," Oliver Wendell Holmes' "The Last
   Leaf," Christina Rosetti's "When I am Dead,
   My Dearest," A. E. Houseman's "Loveliest of
   Trees," Dylan Thomas' "Do Not Go Gentle
   Into That Good Night," Bronte's "Fall,
   Leaves, Fall," Sara Teasdale's "Leaves" and
   Shakespeare's "Seven Ages of Man." And a
   story you might like is O. Henry's "The Last
   Leaf." How do these compare with the film?
8. Air and water currents, aging and gravity,
   are some of the forces which shape the leaf's
   cycle. If you relate the leaf to a human being, what forces shape the course of a person's journey through life?
9. How many verbs can you discover to fit the
   actions of the leaf and the actions of animals and other elements in the film?

65

0. Before showing the film, you might want to run it through, without the projection lamp on, playing merely the sound track. What's your impression of the music?
1. Show the film without the sound track. Instead, play Simon and Garfunkel's "Sound of Silence," "Wish I was a Kellogg's Cornflake," or "Old People." How does a different sound track affect the film? Try it with any other record.

HOW *LEAF* WAS MADE:

Fred Hudson and two other members of a camera crew spent three weeks in Yosemite National Park filming *Leaf.* Fred shot most of the film with a Bolex 16mm camera, using a shooting ratio of about 10 to one (a foot of film was used out of every 10 shot). Fred commented that, "if you try to work *with*, instead of against, nature, it is a lot easier." Things seemed to go well with this film.

The major job of one crew member was to drop leaves from the top of a cliff. Daily, leaves were gathered; over 100 leaves were used to make the film. The thermal wind currents would be tested several times, then a leaf would be shot. There were several very lucky shots, according to Fred. "The gods were smiling," he commented. "Something else was working for us. That something else was superlative." In one shot, for example, a leaf moved to the side of a huge rock, and seemed to linger and kiss it.

The whole film was shot in slow motion, a fact which does not seem apparent to most viewers. The camera ran at 60 frames per second as compared with the normal 24 frames per second.

Leaf was intended to be part of a longer film that has not been made entitled *The October Nut.* It is a photoplay story about an insane man who feels that if he can escape to the sea shore in autumn, a divine revelation will appear, fetters will dissolve, and he will be free. One day, he escapes. Chased by his keepers, he reaches the sea. There he has a fantasy. He is a leaf, freed from what has bound him. He finds relief in the fantasy that tells his story. He is fulfilled and exhausted by it. Then he is caught and returned to the asylum, but something has been revealed to him. He has changed.

Leaf, then, was intended to be the fantasy of the madman.

Fred Hudson intended to film *Leaf* in a more complex manner, using superimpositions, simultaneous shots from different angles, and other sophisticated film techniques. Budget limitations, plus the fact that Fred was the only cameraman, forced him to use the simpler approach. It is probable that the seemingly harsh limitation was actually a blessing, for the deceptive simplicity evokes a curious power in its metaphor.

67

The lovely circular pan of leaves on the trees against the sky was shot by placing the camera on a tire and pushing it down the stream. The leaf floating into the darkness of the shadow was actually floating out of it and printed backwards.

There were, however, no phoney tricks in the film, such as strings. The leaves used actually floated and performed as they were shot.

Fred Hudson, artist and perfectionist that he is, considers *Leaf* a simple exercise, where he attempted to show the invisible world of air as it affected the leaf. Others have found the film much more than that—a simple, beautifully rendered visual poem that lingers in the eye of the mind.

DUNES

A film produced by David Adams.
Filmed and edited by Fred Hudson.
Music by Michele Michelet
Time: 7 min.; Color,
Distributed by Pyramid

Dunes is another poetic description of a natural cycle, with emphasis on specific imagery. It contrasts the sweeping, changing contours of sand dunes in varying tones of light with the effects of the environment on animals that inhabit the desert.

Dunes opens with an optical rendition of sunrise over the sand dunes. The image of the sun grows larger. Then we see the sunrise reflected on the striking contours and undulating shapes of the dunes. After various, stunning shots of these shapes, we see a close-up of a scorpion. The camera zooms backward and the scorpion meanders along, leaving its tracks in the sand. Next we see a sidewinder snake slithering along the sand, suggesting, in its movements, the dunes themselves. The next shot is of grass, wavering in the wind.

A kangaroo rat, in close-up, nibbles on a blade of grass. Then we see a sand beetle, tiny against the expanse, scurrying along the sand.

A long backward zoom of another snake is captivating as its track makes an artistic design, intersecting with the lines of the sand.

The wind rises, sand blows. In quick succession, we see close-ups of a tarantula, a fringed-foot lizard, grass bending in the increasing force of the wind, then a tumbleweed, loping down a hill.

Feeling the impending storm, the lizard darts across the sand, the tumbleweed tumbles faster, then the sand begins to blow very hard. The snake moves against the force of the wind. The beetle and the snake rush for cover.

The sandstorm becomes almost blinding. The tarantula constricts its legs, the lizard burrows under the sand, while the scorpion finds shelter under a sand ledge.

We watch the power and grandeur of the storm as the sand blows and shifts the shapes of the dunes, and the grass bends in the force of the wind. The kangaroo rat is buffeted.

The sand moves swiftly across the dunes like waves of water pouring over an angry sea of desert.

Soon the storm stops. The lizard peeps from its burrow, the tumbleweed again ambles lazily along with a gentle breeze. Soon the other animals desert their shelters in the peace of the dying light.

sand floats in the golden breeze. As sunset approaches, we see the rat against the red sun, and shadows begin to cover the smooth, stationary waves of sand. All is golden and day is dying. In a close-up shot, the rat digs in the sand. As dusk falls, we see the tarantula, walking across the top of a dune, back lit by an enormous glowing sunset.

The optical image of the sunset, gradually diminishing, ends the picture.

AFTER THE FILM:

Dunes, aside from the stunning beauty of the sand shapes themselves, is unusual in that it shows the lives of normally repulsive or unattractive animals as they struggle to survive the force of the storm. The animals become individual characters that draw our sympathy through their struggles. They even become beautiful through the naturalness of their actions and reactions. Fred Hudson's precise eye and poetic feeling for nature achieve a haunting impact. He shows us an alien world where the force of nature is indifferent to living things, and survival is the watchword.

1. Imagine yourself stranded in the desert as the storm approaches. Describe what you experience.
2. Tell the story of *Dunes* from the points of view of the various animals. What precise images and specific actions can you remember?
3. Write a *haiku,* or a poem in another form, about the theme of the film.
4. How does *Dunes* show cause-and-effect relationships?
5. Compare the desert of dunes with the moods and shapes of the sea.
6. Research the topic of sand dunes.
7. How does *Dunes* illustrate the indifference of nature?

8. You might want to find poetry or literature about experiences with the desert or sand dunes.

HOW *DUNES* WAS MADE:

Dunes was entirely shot and edited by Fred Hudson, off and on over a period of about a year and a half. It was filmed in three different locations—the Pismo Dunes of Southern California, Death Valley, and in the sand hills of southeastern California near Yuma, Arizona.

The animals in the picture were "professional actors," accompanied by a trainer who had a feeling for their individual personalities. Originally, there were two kangaroo rats, one larger than the other. On the trip to the location, the smaller one killed the larger one (these animals have to continually gnaw on grass or something like it. If deprived, they attack each other, since they are cannibalistic.) The Pismo Dunes are close to the sea and the sea air made the animals sluggish and uncooperative. The trainer was particularly unhappy with the scorpion because it would not take direction. In fact, he wanted to kill the scorpion. Artistic temperaments flare during films—even animal films.

The animals are indigenous to the region, but Fred Hudson doubts if they would act as they do in the film during a sandstorm. They would probably be too smart to be caught in it. Thus the story is fabricated, according to Fred, as it often is in film art.

Fred Hudson made the following comments about his intent in making the film and the problems he encountered:

"In the wild world, the world that is not peopled, not manned, I don't think I've ever yet been anywhere . . . whether it's a desert, a mountain, wherever it is—there is always some moment in the day or night that is ultra-magical, bigger than life. I can't say this about the human world. There are too many days, too many times, when nothing magical transpires, nothing that is gracious, that shows dignity or poetry or anything else.

73

I think we should take advantage of this wonderful thing that we have . . . the sort of thing that helps man to be bigger than himself. He has to go away from men to experience it. And when he comes back he is a head higher.

I don't mean this in any terms of fantasy or escape. This is hard-core reality, and hard-core reality has greatness in it. It is uplifting.

There is a sort of golden moment in time and it is always there at some time in a period of 24 hours, no matter where you are in the wild world. More often than not, it occurs more than once a day. Thoreau had a lot to imply about this in his writings.

In *Dunes,* I was working for a golden moment in time—it was that moment, to me, where the desert land is transformed into a magical playground, just 10 minutes before that sun dips behind the great sand world.

You just can't describe it. Something just happens. It is very fleeting.

The idea was great. I was getting all kinds of these beautiful golden long shots, and yet it turned out that I just did not have a film. I mean I recorded this very accurately—this golden moment—so what do you do about it? I figured that the honest thing would be to have one long scene called the golden moment in time. It would have one scene—just one scene long. But I realized that I wanted to have a film—build a film, so I tried to devise whatever I could with the inanimate world of sand that showed this strangeness, the other world that would lead into the golden moment.

And even that was not enough. It was a short vignette or exercise. I realized I had to get some meat on the bones. Then I happened on the idea of animals—those animals that are part of the sand world. Let's have a look at them, too. That still was not enough. I had to devise some kind of plot. The plot would be an action plot that the eyeball and the mind would have no trouble looking at and experiencing. Then I hit upon a windstorm, another element in nature that works in conflict with this. That is what I did.

I still hope that everything added together does unify—has a feeling that there is a strange, golden, quiet, wonderful, fleeting moment in time. We should look for these more often.

All those things were to serve that—the windstorm, the animals, the ripples in the sand, the design. It was all to serve that feeling that now we're at the golden moment, now it is at hand."

WATERS OF YOSEMITE

A film produced by David Adams.
Filmed and edited by Fred Hudson.

Award of Merit—Edinburgh
International Film Festival

Time: 9 min.; Color

Distributed by Pyramid

Waters of Yosemite is a splash of beauty, a poem to the delicacy and brute force of water in its many forms. Fred Hudson's intent was to capture the magical variety of a crystal clear river as it progresses downward from its quiet source, gradually building power, reaching a climax, receding, then building up force again.

The film begins with a quiet scene, while we hear the voice of Joseph Wood Krutch, the eminent naturalist and conservationist, who says: "One of the commonest of everyday miracles, an icicle that was once water, is turning back into water again. This is a poem about running water—a poem in pictures, not in words. It says something about one particular stream in Yosemite National Park, and at the same time, something about the wild, wilful beauty of all streams that are free to flow as nature made them."

An idyllic scene is presented, where the water flows, causing a shower of water like rain. We see the sunlight glimmering on the water. The flow increases, the force builds, until we see billows as the water cascades over cliffs, churning and thrashing.

Shapes and contours are shown in striking close-ups as it reaches roaring rapids. High-flying spray shoots out and falls like wild dust, until a climax seems to be achieved.

Then we see the soft mist of water, droplets close up on tree leaves as the mist drifts over the rocks. Trees are backlit by the sun, drops form on branches and grass blades, and a feeling of peace prevails.

Then the power builds again until the water becomes a boiling mass of white explosions, smashing over rocks in clouds and torrents of grandeur. In the mist over the raging whiteness, hangs a rainbow, and we see close-ups of the tempest—fury in the late afternoon.

At the end of the film, Joseph Wood Krutch says: "In wildness is a whole beautiful world for man to admire—to think about—and sometimes, alas, to destroy. No nation in the world is richer than ours in what are called natural resources. But we sometimes forget that beauty also is one of the resources, and that it should be valued and conserved, as much a resource as any other.

To realize this, we need only to have eyes to see and ears to hear. Poetry, whether in words or in pictures, opens our eyes and opens our hearts. The next time we see a flowing stream, let us remember how this poet saw and felt the waters of Yosemite."

with the other films, Fred Hudson's needle e catches the subtle tones and shapes, the riety of movement and power of the water as flows and goes through its astounding meta- orphoses. Close-ups catch and follow leaping, otean shapes, the reflections and the bom- rdments of natural force. The film is a feast r the eyes, making us aware of the wild force d peace that one stream assumes in the soli- de of wilderness.

FTER THE FILM:

How did this film affect you? Did you find it poetic?
What images did you see in the film?
You might like to write about other natural phenomena such as wind, fire, or clouds.
Find a record or tape which will substitute for the film's sound track.
Play the record of Debussy's "La Mer." As you listen to it, write impressions into a poem, composition or film.
Compare the water scenes in *Why Man Creates* and *The Searching Eye* with the scenes in *Waters of Yosemite*.
How does the sand in *Dunes* compare with the water in this film?

OW *WATERS OF YOSEMITE* WAS MADE:

aters of Yosemite was shot, at various times, ver a period of six months in Yosemite National ark. Fred Hudson considers Yosemite the great ater spectacle place of the universe. Weather as the major problem since he wanted to catch clear, spring-like quality. Sometimes he would e socked in for a week with gray days.

Fred made these comments about the filming:

"I tried to catch the magic in water—the vari- ety—to accent some of the nuances that would require close study. You have to live with it, to be around it, really observe it. There are real- ly some rare things. I sort of feel I just scratch- ed the surface of some of the textures, the mys- tery movements.

There is a wide world of things hardly seen that the camera can see—single out. For example, the high-speed camera giving extreme slow mo- tion, the ultra-close-up lens—would reveal things not seen in my film. I was using normal techni- ques to photograph the glints and dances of mountain and river water. I tried to make a unit that was more than a passing glance at things.

I once did a poor film in college called *Water.*
Then I did a black-and-white film called *River.*

In *Waters of Yosemite,* patterned after *River* I
alternated climax and quiescence. All three films
were based on one of John Muir's essays. He
was the great conservationist who said about
one of the rivers in Yosemite: 'It moves like a
wild animal, full of the strength of the mountains and the huge wild joy.'

I wanted to get a wild, animal-like quality, joy-
ous, strong that alternately gathered and ex-
pended its forces."

Although *Waters of Yosemite* is his favorite film,
at this time, Fred Hudson feels that some of the
shots are too long. Certainly, the film's impact
is dazzling and it makes a strong argument for
conserving our natural resources.

AUTUMN: FROST COUNTRY

A film produced by David Adams.
Filmed and edited by Fred Hudson.
Conceived and written by David A. Sohn.
"Best Ten" Award—Photographic
Society of America
Time: 9 min.; Color
Distributed by Pyramid

Autumn: Frost Country combines the precise eyes of two sensitive poets: Robert Frost and Fred Hudson. Robert Frost's words from his poem "The Road Not Taken" signal the beginning of a journey. His poem "Reluctance" completes the excursion. Fred Hudson's film captures Frost's environment as he might have seen it.

The film carries us, with the use of dissolves, through the captivating country of Vermont and other New England scenes where Robert Frost made his home. There are many visual allusions to Frost's poetry, such as birches, a mending wall, and a spider web. The film catches Frost's feeling for the woods and other elements of nature as it illustrates some major thematic areas of Frost's vision: the movement from light to darkness, the progression from general to specific, and the emphasis on common aspects of the world around him which served as something more in his skillful metaphors.

The film is a visual metaphor for the verbal metaphors that frame it. Besides affording insights into Robert Frost's world, the film is a pleasing experience for the eye, floating through the bright glory of autumn in a New England countryside.

AFTER THE FILM:

1. What does Frost's "The Road Not Taken" and "Reluctance" say to you? Other poems you might like to read are "Mending Wall," "The Sound of Trees," "Birches," and "Design."
2. Can you describe precisely some of the images you discovered in the film?
3. Compare Robert Frost's writing with that of Thoreau, Emerson, Whitman, Bryant, Howard Nemerov, Robert Francis, and Dylan Thomas.
4. Play a recording of Frost reading his poetry and devise your own visuals to accompany the words.
5. Visit a park, woods or other natural area. Could you translate your experience to paper or film?
6. Compare and contrast the original script treatment of the film (which follows) with the film itself.

HOW *AUTUMN: FROST COUNTRY* WAS MADE:

My intention in writing the film script was to catch the spirit of Frost's vision through a visual examination of his environment and poetry. In using poetry with film one must guard against telling the viewer what he is seeing. Such films as *Morning on the Lievre* and *Hangman* have successfully skirted the danger.

At one point, we almost included "My November Guest" at about midpoint in the film. An argument for it was that it would give a clearer view of Frost's feelings about such a trip. The argument against it was that it would destroy the visual context by intruding with words. We decided to use only the two poems since we felt that they acted as framing devices to accent the whole visual progression.

On working with Fred Hudson before he went to Vermont to shoot the film, I stressed that: (1) the film should move gradually from light to darkness, this being a recurrent theme of Robert Frost's, (2) there should be many progressions from general to specific in visual images, as this was a pattern that Frost frequently followed. Finally, I felt that the film should help the viewer experience Frost's environment. Fred Hudson read much of Frost's poetry. He returned from New England with 80 minutes of film which I examined about 10 times, finally learning the

shots in the film. I took notes and used a tape recorder to describe each shot. Then I made rough suggestions to Fred for editing. He followed many, but not all of them. I felt that he should be the final judge of what really worked in the context of what we were trying to do.

David Adams the producer, and Fred Hudson decided to use long dissolves between shots to make the film seem to move at a leisurely pace and also to give it a soft, illusory quality. Most dissolves are 48 frames long, but in this film, Fred used dissolves of 96 or 128 frames. The shooting ratio was about 10 to one.

I searched for a sound track that would fit. After listening to many records, I felt that Eric Satie's "Trois Gymnopedies" (Orchestrated by Debussy) had the soft, dreamlike, cool quality that would fit the film without intruding.

SCRIPT OF *AUTUMN: FROST COUNTRY*

The film begins with long shots of the pastel woods, coming closer, while the title appears: *Autumn: Frost Country* (sound track: simple flute or recorder).

In the 59 seconds during which Frost reads "The Road Not Taken," there are various shots of predominantly yellow and orange foliage, no music.

Music. Camera tracks under yellow trees along road. Cut to forest; several shots of foliage— backward zoom reveals burnt-orange leaves; shots establish mood of woods; zoom in on red maple.

Close-up: leaves and branches. Lots of color. One dead leaf hanging, ready to drop. Wind whips across reflected sunlight giving turbulent sea effect. Shots of falling leaves.

Cut to static "pastel painting" shot of stream. Shot of brown moving water, with curved dots of light. Zoom in on rippling waves. Medium shot of falling rain. Cut to reflected trees, then posts. Pan down to abstract images in rippling water.

85

Medium shot of ducks moving first right, then left. Ending with shot of ducks; blue sky reflected at right of frame.

Pan through birches and beech. Medium shot of clumps; close-up of peeling bark. Shot of birches; focus shifts from foreground to background to foreground, giving dreamlike effect. Out-of-focus zoom in on red berries. Shot of milkweed pod; zoom to specific pods, moving in wind. Close-ups of dead Queen Anne's lace. Shot of pine branch overhanging water.

Medium shot of two buck deer; of fawns.

Variety of tree shots, backlit. Shot of darker woods. Wall sequence; zoom in and out on rocks and leaves. Fern sequence—backlit—zooming in. Shot of spider web, glistening in the sun. Cut to dark woods, pierced with shaft of light.

Light fades; dark silhouettes of bare trees against the light and clouds. Shot of dark water. Zoom in on light reflections. Music stops.

Shot of archway of trees; snow falls. Camera tracks along road, snow-covered rocks in foreground; trees silhouetted against sun in background. Voice over, poem "Reluctance." END.

CONCLUSION:

The first unit emphasized the need for observation and creativity. The second unit has suggested the importance of a precise eye for images and details. The writer as well as the filmmaker needs to develop the faculty for catching the fleeting images and details and then reconstructing them for the reader or viewer.

One may see with precise eyes, but like Fred Hudson, one must interpret the vision through the filter of one's imagination.

Eye be nimble,
Eye, be quick . . . .

See how they run . . . .

— *Snatches echoing nursery rhymes.*

II. THE INVENTIVE EYE: Impression and Compression

ART
AMERICAN TIME CAPSULE
WORLD OF '68
HOME OF THE BRAVE
DEEP BLUE WORLD

Kinestasis is the animation of still photographs through very fast cutting. It comes from *kine,* meaning "movement" and *stasis,* meaning "stillness." Filmmakers who use this technique visually "shoot the rapids". Photographs, paintings and other visuals are shot with a camera capable of taking single frames. Each image is given from two to 10 frames. A frame stays on the screen for 1/24 of a second. Reading experts say that good readers can absorb three-word phrases flashed on a screen at 1/100th of a second.

Kinestasis has only recently become popular. Arthur Lipsett was one of the first to use the technique in *Very Nice, Very Nice* and other National Film Board of Canada films. Norman McLaren also used quick flash techniques in *Blinkity Blank* and some of his other films. Hugh and Suzanne Johnson of Princeton, New Jersey, made a short kinestasis film for the Westinghouse Corporation entitled *1800 Days* which summed up five years of American history from the late 50's to the early 60's.

Any technique, however, takes time before it is accepted. Eisenstein and D.W. Griffith were on to something like it, but the present mood seems to fit the rapid bombardment of visuals.

The films in this unit trace a quick growth in sophistication in the use of the technique. If you follow the films in sequence, you will see a chunk of history pass before your eyes. Perhaps, too, the visual impact of kinestasis will remind you of some television commercials. They have picked up fast cutting very quickly.

Fast cutting has become more and more popular in both feature and short films in recent years. Jean-Luc Godard virtually eliminated the dissolve technique in feature films when he made *Breathless.* As we pass through the day, we are constantly confronted with a shower of images from billboards, street signs, and rapidly passing objects and people. We are therefore accustomed to fragmentation of imagery and the fleeting glance.

Young people, saturated with television and speed living, respond enthusiastically to fast cutting. Kinestasis is also used to teach number, symbol and other concepts to pre-schoolers on the television series called *Sesame Street.*

The use of these kinestasis films can be excellent training in observation, for the viewer will see more and more in each film as screenings are repeated.

89

90

ART (Or for the first time, 3000 years of fine art in three minutes).

A film by Dan McLaughlin.

Awards: ART was selected by the U.S.I.A. for a world-wide program, "American Independent Film Makers"

Time: 3-1/2 min.; Color

Distributed by Pyramid

Art (originally entitled *God Is Dog Spelled Backwards*) is a quick trip through the world of fine art. Each image was given two frames (1/12th of a second). This adds up to 720 images per minute—or 2160 images in the three-minute film. That's a lot of art in a short time.

The paintings are not necessarily in chronological order, but schools of painting are grouped, so that Oriental art rushes by, early religious paintings, mosaics, the Dutch masters, the Impressionists, cave art, abstract modern paintings and others are briefly on the screen. Blink, and you can miss a whole school.

There are several illusions of movement in the film. Bulls seem to be running in the cave art sequence. Mosaics seem to churn and blend. Streets merge, dancers seem to dance. You will find more of these effects if you watch the film several times. The soundtrack is Beethoven's "Fifth Symphony." The film ends abruptly, and the following message appears.

"You have just had all of the great art in the world indelibly etched on your brain. You are now cultured."

AFTER THE FILM:

1. Did you see the various sequences of schools of art in the film?
2. Did specific paintings impress you after the first showing? Why not look again and see if anything new strikes you.
3. Are you inclined to further investigate the art of the world?
4. How do artists show that they are keen observers? Examine several different artists and see if they have an eye for detail.

HOW *ART* WAS MADE:

Art was made by Dan McLaughlin, head of the animation department at UCLA, in 1963. He was interested in discovering how much a person could perceive if images were exposed very quickly on the screen. In this sense, it is an experimental film. He hit upon the idea of laying out much of the world's great art in a short film, shooting images in random sequence, tending to group certain schools.

94

A person of wry wit, Dan McLaughlin has a classic explanation of the film: "If you take the world's greatest art and combine it with the world's greatest music, you should have the world's greatest film." As an aside, he said that because the "Mona Lisa" was supposed to be the world's greatest painting, he gave her 12 frames, or a half second.

He shot *Art* in his garage in two weeks, satisfied himself with its effect, and put it on the shelf in his garage for three years.

One day, talking to a student about film, Dan mentioned the fast-moving film he had made. It was suggested that he show it to the students. It was shown with a film called *Guilt*. Later, it was shown in Encino, California, and at the Foothill Festival. Its emergence in the film world was actually a fluke.

McLaughlin likes to play with words. Traveling on the freeway one day, he thought of the title, *God Is Dog Spelled Backwards*. He liked it as an attention-getter, a title that would loosen up the audience bearing no relation at all to the film. Later, because of objections the film title was changed to *Art*.

The film was shot with a Bolex, two baby lamps, and a table, upon which he set up the visuals. He shot 100 ft. in two weeks, and then quit. The closing statement was intended satirically. According to Dan McLaughlin, too many people confuse facts with knowledge. All this information can be assimilated very quickly, but such an exposure does not make a person knowledgeable. The film does have an emotional impact on some people.

The only editing was the cutting out of George Washington, who appeared more than once.

McLaughlin does not like the word kinestasis, which he thinks is a "put-on" word. He prefers the term "iconic graphic." He had not seen the films of Arthur Lipsett when he made *Art*. He arrived at the concept separately which is the type of "fooling around" that *Why Man Creates* suggests may lead to a viable idea. *Art* was actually the inspiration for Charles Braverman's *American Time Capsule*.

95

MERICAN TIME CAPSULE

film by Charles Braverman.

ecial Chairman's Award,
·ld Camera, U.S. Industrial Film
stival

·ne: 3 min.; Color

stributed by Pyramid

nerican Time Capsule captures 200 years of
merican history in three minutes. Each visual
the film was held from 1/12th to 2/3rds of
second. Originally, the film was made for the
nothers Brothers' Comedy Hour.

·e film is developed in chronological order,
·ginning with the Revolutionary War and end-
·g with President Nixon. Sequences include
·ashington, Franklin, the Constitutional Con-
·ntion, Indian fighting, covered wagons, Andrew
·ckson, slavery and others. There is then an
·xtended sequence on the Civil War, Confede-
·te scenes, Negro soldiers, Grant, Lee, Sher-
·an, Lincoln's assassination, the conspirators
·anged, and the Klu Klux Klan.

·e then see the winning of the West—Indian
·ghting, Western heroes such as Custer, Wild
·ll Hickok and others, then riverboats, Huckle-
·erry Finn and early cities.

·he film then touches upon important inven-
·ons; World War I; Mickey Mouse; and other
·nages leading into World War II.

·he film was cut to the drum solo of Sandy Nel-
·on. It begins with a slower tom-tom beat and
·radually increases in speed and intensity, build-
·ng to a climax.

·he film was carefully designed to give illusions
·f movement. Horses seem to draw wagons,
·owboys ride across the screen, the Wright
·3rothers fly the first airplane, soldiers fight,

and World War I pilots have dogfights in the air.
The use of zooms and panning with the camera
add variety and realism to the film.

The film makes one realize how much of our
history has been concerned with war.

AFTER THE FILM:

1. Did you notice the design of the film?
2. What are your impressions of American history as seen through the film?
3. In your opinion, does the film have a point
   of view?

4. Compare and contrast the technique and the
   impact of this film with "The Edifice" sequence in *Why Man Creates.*

HOW *AMERICAN TIME CAPSULE* WAS MADE:

Because of the related nature of *American Time
Capsule* and *World of '68*, the making of the two
films is discussed after the material on *World
of '68.*

 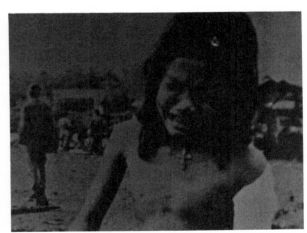

WORLD OF '68

film by Charles Braverman.
Photographed by Sylvia Dees.
Production Assistant: Ken Rudolph
Gold Medal Award—Atlanta
International Film Festival
Time: 4-1/2 min.; Color
Distributed by Pyramid

World of '68, encompassing the significant events of that year, was made for the Smothers Brothers' Comedy Hour and was also shown on a CBS News Broadcast.

Unlike American Time Capsule, this film is not strictly chronological. It differs also in that moving picture newsclips are inter-cut with still photographs. The effect is a mosaic of events summing up the violence, laughter, action, and spirit of the year.

The film includes shots of the Vietnam conflict, the Biafran crisis, the Columbia riots, the assassinations of Martin Luther King, Jr., and Robert Kennedy.

The sound track is by the Iron Butterfly, with guitar overlays. The music begins with a slow beat and picks up speed to match the visuals.

AFTER THE FILM:

1. Would you have changed American Time Capsule or World of '68 in any way?
2. How would you make a film on another year — past or future?
3. If you feel ambitious, make a kinestasis film. (See the article on "How to Make a Kinestasis Film".) You might try to catch the spirit of a city, or a school year, for example.

HOW AMERICAN TIME CAPSULE AND WORLD OF '68 WERE MADE:

The first kinestasis film by Charles Braverman, American Time Capsule, resulted from a meeting between Braverman and Tommy Smothers. Charles Braverman had seen Art and felt that a kinestasis short might be a welcome addition to the Smothers Brothers' Comedy Hour. Tommy Smothers suggested a film on the history of sculpture, but Charles Braverman felt it might not interest the audience. He hit upon the idea of a quick overview of about 200 years of U.S. history in three minutes. The audience response to American Time Capsule was enthusiastic. About 35 million people saw the film—a healthy audience for any premiere.

After the success of the first film, the Smothers Brothers commissioned World of '68. When first shown two days before President Nixon's election the final shot in the Presidents' sequence was a question mark. Nixon's picture was added later.

Charles Braverman said in an interview:

"To make American Time Capsule I first gathered the materials, in no special order. The equipment was basic: a single frame, 16mm reflex camera, Mickey Mouse illegitimate type of horizontal animation stand, and a modest lighting set-up.

First, I spent a couple of days looking for the sound track. I knew generally what I wanted to get, and after listening to an awful lot of records, I found what I wanted. I edited that down. Then I counted the number of frames in between each beat, and I knew that I wanted each scene to correspond with each beat. I couldn't control the music because I didn't have enough money to write a score, but I found the music that I

liked and after editing that, I knew that I wanted each scene to change on the beat of the music. So I had the music transferred to 16mm magnetic film and I counted the frames in between each beat of the music so I knew how many frames it would be for each scene.

Then we began filming in a garage, one frame at a time. It took us four or five nights, six, seven, or eight hours a night until morning.

I think that the best way I communicate and the best way that I can encourage people to think is by making films.

I had a point of view in *American Time Capsule,* but it is not a propaganda film. Basically it looks at the history of the United States in a condensed, fast form, and it has strange, powerful impact because when you look at two hundred years in three minutes, you see things that maybe you didn't realize before.

I read as many as possible of the letters to the Smothers Brothers from people who saw the film. A large number of liberals thought it was a great anti-war film while those on the right wing thought it was a patriotic, flag-waving film. Some people said that there was too much war in the film. Maybe they mean there has been too much war in the history of the United States.

World of '68 and *American Time Capsule* look alike to most people, but the techniques are totally different. The only thing that was similar technically was that I had tracks first. I had two different record cuts, and a musician friend did guitar overlays over one of the cuts.

All the still material was picked out in advance, cut out, and mounted on punched animation paper. The film was really made when I wrote the animation exposure sheets.

Besides being completely pre-planned, *World of '68* was better technically because it was shot n a $25,000 Oxberry animation stand. So the zooms and other moves are smoother. I also included motion picture film clips.

One thing that I'm proud of with *World of '68* is that except for the World Series, every single major event of 1968 is there. After the film was finished, someone pointed out the missing element.

My two assistants on *World of '68* were Ken Rudolph who did the bulk of the research, and Sylvia Dees who did the filming. I put everything together and wrote the exposure sheets. That's

where the film was directed, by sitting down for ten days and writing the exposure sheets, a frame at a time.

World of '68 gets a more emotional reaction than *American Time Capsule* because of what happened in 1968. Even though the Civil War was a long drawn-out thing and there were an awful lot of people killed in it, it doesn't have

the same emotional impact because it didn't affect us directly.

After *World of '68,* a lot of people wanted me to do kinestasis films on the history of whatever product they were pushing, and things like that. But I like to keep trying to do different things. I am now producing an hour-long TV special that is a *cinema verité* documentary, which was originally my interest before I made a kinestasis film.

As for the technique of kinestasis, it's a great way for someone to make a film without spending very much money. I think it has a place in film. It's only one aspect of many things you can do with film, and it's an exciting technique. It's a way of showing a lot of things, or many aspects of the same thing, in a very short time."

HOME OF THE BRAVE

A film produced by David Adams.
Written and directed by Michael Bloebaum.

Photography by Charles Satterfield.

Time: 3 min.; Color

Distributed by Pyramid

Home of The Brave is a kinestasis film with live-action clips that encompasses the history of the American Indian from pre-Spanish times to today.

In the section on how *Home of The Brave* was made, Michael Bloebaum explains that the intent of the film was to capture in condensed form the virtual disappearance of the Indian cultures through what the white man has called progress.

AFTER THE FILM:

1. Research the story of the American Indians in depth.
2. What are your reactions to the film?
3. Can you think of any ways in which the Indian cultures have affected our own?
4. Discuss *Why Man Creates* in relation to this film. Could this film be entitled *How Man Destroys?*
5. Have you visited an Indian reservation? What was your impression of it?
6. Discuss the demise of the Indian cultures and the treatment of Indians in relation to other races and cultures that have undergone similar treatment.
7. You might want to compare *American Time Capsule* with *Home of The Brave.* You could even show them both at once on two projectors.

105

HOW *HOME OF THE BRAVE* WAS MADE:

Michael Bloebaum described it as follows:

"David Adams and I had talked about doing a kinestasis film on California history, but I thought the Indians of the West would be a more interesting topic. He liked that.

I researched a number of books and got some photos from them. Then I shot a live-action sequence of a young Indian in the thought that using live footage along with stills would get the meaning across a little more subtly. Showing the Indian contemplating a sunset is an abstract rather than a literal sequence that represents the coming of the missionaries to the West. All my research indicated that the Indians were quite receptive to the white man when they first came, and they were very friendly and, basically, very peaceful. So, as the missionary appears, the Indian smiles at him and the camera zooms in on the cross. Then the film cuts to the stills of crosses from various missions in California and scenes from those missionary days, with a sound track of mission bells.

I use the Indian drum throughout, except near the end, where I substitute the heartbeat because it seems to me that the life has been sapped from the Indian, and I didn't think the drum would be appropriate at that point.

I also discovered that the American Revolution was quite important in the opening of the West, because the United States gained its independence and set all those energies free to expand westward.

Of course, with the greater expansion westward, the Indian was pushed from his native lands and his native way of living. My film illustrates how basically the white man infused his own type of violence, and forced the Indian to react with that same type of violence in trying to protect his lands and property.

Then comes the sequence of the United States leaders—Washington, Adams, Clay and Polk, contrasted with the Indian leaders, Tecumseh, Red Fox, and Geronimo. The drumbeat picks up to a war-like beat.

The Gold Rush sequence which follows shows the American pioneers shooting Indians as they would shoot animals—for the fun of it.

I also suggest some of the raucous ways of life in the Gold Rush era. And you'll notice that the shots of the Indians are fewer and when the Indians move they move away from the camera. This suggests that the Indian is still being moved away from his homeland, and the place he had inhabited for so many years.

I think the sound track of 'Clementine' is appropriate because it was one of the tunes popular in the Gold Rush period.

The rhythm of the drums matches closely the rhythm of the train. You'll notice that I show some movement in the train sequence stills. For example, near the end of the sequence, there's one zoom to an Indian's eyes and two shots of an Indian woman. In the last shot of her, she goes out of focus, suggesting the Indian's being pushed, not only away from his homeland, but also out of civilization's focus. Not only was his civilization taken from him, he was not around to participate in ours.

The train sequence ends quickly, bringing us up to contemporary times. Live footage of freeway traffic and an oil well is intercut with stills.

This conveys the idea that man and his civilization has basically perverted and polluted what was a very pastoral way of life.

There's another transition shot from underneath the oil well as the arm comes down with the sun. Then we cut to the sun, and down at the ghost town of Bodie, California. This sequence, with distorted 'Clementine' music behind it, is meant to indicate that all the pioneers and Gold Rush people are gone and forgotten.

The film cuts to the Indian reservation and we hear the sound of the heartbeat. Through this juxtaposition, I'm saying that ghost town, pioneer and Indian, too, have been forgotten. The Indian *is* a forgotten man in our society. He still lives, though in very poor circumstances. You can see it in the picture of the old Indian on the reservation. He doesn't even have a roof over his head. He has an old broken-down bed and some pots and pans for cooking.

Home of The Brave shows the Indian as a man of great dignity. As he knew happiness before the white man, he was happy. He didn't live a perfect life as we regard a perfect life today, but he was happy. The white man not only corrupted him but at the same time pushed him from his homeland into the desert, where he lives today. He was not even permitted to fend for himself.

I tried to say that the Indian has always looked at the white man's activity—his coming West—while standing apart from it, in a way. True, he fought, but the basic Indian code is one of stoicism. I have a lot of shots of Indians' faces which show this."

DEEP BLUE WORLD

A film by Sylvia Dees. Produced by
David Adams
Time: 7 min.; Color
Distributed by Pyramid

The concept of *Deep Blue World* is exciting,
and the techniques so original that it is a spectacular film.

According to Sylvia Dees: "The idea of the film
is one of adventure. It's a trip to the deep blue
world. Your mind is going to be expanded by the
film. This is more than just a factual recording
of what's down there beneath the surface of the
water. That would be yawn-making material. It's
an adventure, an exploration. You can see beautiful things in almost a fantasy way.

One of the influences on the film has been the
recent landings on the moon. I've been thinking
about it—the sort of excitement that has been
generated all over the world. A lot of people
have been talking about the fact that there aren't
any more frontiers to explore. We've done them
all, and the only ones you can do now are out
in space. Of course, that requires millions of
dollars, great teams of scientists, and not just
any one of us can qualify to be an astronaut.
We kind of go along with them vicariously, but
we can't physically do it.

But there's one thing that has been really over-
looked. Most of the land areas have been explored, more or less. There may be some of
them farther out, places high up in the mountains, desert areas that haven't been completely gone over, but most of the places that people can get to fairly easily have all been covered.
You're not the first person there, you're the 50th
person, or the 100th. Even if you climb a mountain, you're not the first person up that mountain. But under the sea—it's like people have
forgotten about it. It's a brand new world, and it
hasn't all been explored, and you never know
what you are going to find there. To me, it's
the last frontier that we can go and see—because mere mortals can get scuba gear or even
little face masks and go under the water. And
when you are under water, it's just like going
into space—you're in a different world. It's a
silent world, like the world out in space. It's
very quiet. You don't hear anything, except maybe a breathing apparatus.

A lot of people who have explored unknown
territories, like in the 19th century, write about
how they reacted to it—the awe, and the wonder,
the joy, the beauty that they felt in finding and
discovering these beautiful things. A range of
mountains that no one has ever seen, or exploring the North Pole. Well, you can get the same
feeling under the water. You don't know what
there's going to be, and futhermore, the land-
scape changes. It's not the same all of the time.
There are animals, there are plants, there are
architectural formations made out of minerals
and corals.

Structurally, the film starts out with a scene all in deep blues. There are divers going down, and things going down—downness is the first part of it. And then, the second sequence is kind of mysterious. On the sound track, we'll have music, consisting of multiple recordings and electronic effects. I may use part of Debussy's "La Mer," but electronically twiddled around with so it won't be recognizable—again, I don't want to get stuck in a fuddy-duddy trap—but it does have some sections that lend themselves to a sort of lyricism, harp arpeggios and things.

The second part is mysterious—the mystery of the underwater ocean. What strange things are lurking behind the rocks? Sometimes a little animal will dart out, or maybe a manta ray, or a funny-looking crab.

Then comes a third sequence, with music to match. Again, it's fairly slow, with pans this time, fairly close on the beauties of the underwater world. It's almost as if you're swimming around there, and you can see beautiful coral formations, and sea anemones that are like flowers, and the kind of beauty and gloriousness of it all.

Now the tempo picks up, the filmic tempo. It gets faster—the cutting—it's cut to music—it's building up into more and more color as the film goes on. It started out blue. The lyrical section is just pastels and colors. Now the colors start getting wild. There are bright flashes of coral and weird orange little fishes and red fishes and yellow ones. It's as if you're getting excited at these things you see.

Then it turns into a purely psychedelic section in which there are lots and lots of flashes, and color, and excitement, and brightness. It's sort of a real mind-opener. I can't quite describe it because it's a visual thing. It generates this great feeling of excitement. The forms come out very quickly—sometimes it's done with quick cuts

from one shape to another shape, that all resemble one another very strongly—a radial form, like a starfish might then become a prickly underwater thing, and then it might become something that's sort of a giant ball, little prickly tufts going out, like the thing explodes—then there might be diagonals—a whole sequence of diagonals.

It comes about 3/4 of the way through the movie, and it's the climax of the film. At the end of the film, we move upward into the blue again, but we never go above the water. We've just taken a trip through the deep blue world."

AFTER THE FILM:

1. How would you describe the various moods of the film? Could you write about it?
2. Describe worlds you have seen through the microscope, the telescope, or camera kaleidoscope.
3. What unusual filmic techniques did you notice in the movie?
4. How is it similar to, and how is it different from, other underwater films you may have seen?

HOW *DEEP BLUE WORLD* WAS MADE:

Sylvia Dees talks about making the film:

"It started out with a gigantic mess of 2-1/4 x 2-1/4 and 35mm negatives. I had these blown up into 8 x 10's and 4 x 5's. These were transparencies. I think there were about 12 different photographers on the project.

I put the transparencies under my animation stand and I pan around on them, and truck, and do animation magic. And I also have some special lenses which put in kind of wiggly effects— and gels, and filters, and I turn it into a motion picture with the animation stand. I have complete control of every frame, and I can zoom in critically, fast or slow, but there's also another motion. A motion in time. Now, I can, with animation, do a series of cuts back and forth, and do it much quicker. In the psychedelic sequence, which is very wild and weird, I took original black and white photographs and I had 8 x 10 in. transparencies made. I put gels over them to shoot them with, and they flash in all kinds of different, crazy colors—and I also had a positive made of the same photograph, so I can either combine them in any two colors, or I can reverse them from positive to negative at a moment's notice. It's like being able to do my own opticals, for free.

As far as I know, I'm the only person who likes to work with bottom lights. Normally animation is shot with top lights. Usually animation is made from drawings—on cells or on pieces of paper, pictures from a magazine, or something—and they are lit from the top at a 45-degree angle from two separate lights. I much prefer to work

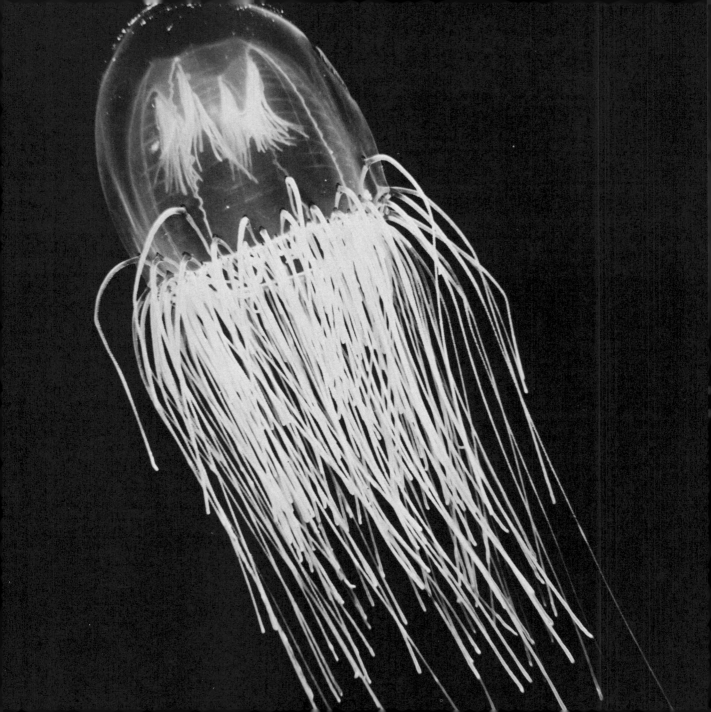

with a light box underneath the machine, and I have converted and jacked it up to 3200 degrees Kelvin, which is the same film temperature that I am shooting it at. Using ordinary light bulbs, and a converter, I make the light bulbs the same color temperature as the film. Their light is projected upward onto a plexiglass plate which diffuses the light. I place the transparency over the plate. Of course, the room is dark, so there are no reflections bouncing around to pick up in the lens. I think the reason nobody else does it is that it's a lot of trouble and it's hard. I like it because you can get very dense blacks that you can't get any other way.

Another trick I like to use a lot is multiple exposure. I can get maybe two decent looking multiple exposures together on the same frame with top light. But if the original material is prepared properly, with a nice, dense black, then I use bottoms—there's no limit to the number of multiple exposures you can get. I've gotten up to about 30 multiple exposures on one frame, and the blacks are still dense. As far as I know, I am the only person who does it this way. I may be giving away some trade secrets, I don't know.

Whenever I make a film, I have an audience in mind. I think the ideal film-goer, the one that's really turned on and excited, whose mind is open, is of college age or the last couple of years of high school. As a matter of fact, this particular audience is not only the most perceptive—their perceptions are much more turned on than those of older people—but their perceptions, because they've had experience in life, are quicker than those of very young people. I have

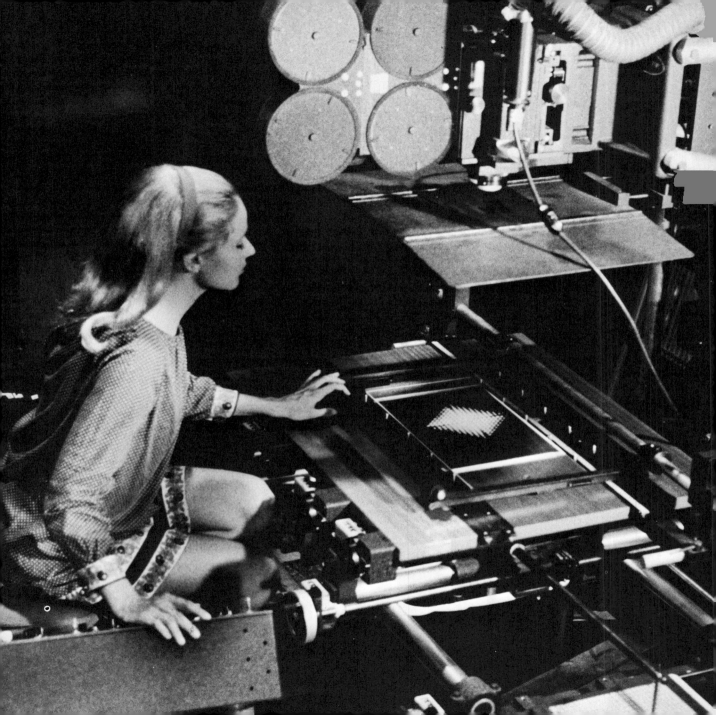

a whole series of timings based on the fact that keen young minds at the peak of their perceptions are going to be seeing this.

The quick-cut film is the kind of film kids are used to seeing. Most educational films are just lousy. I had to sit through a few of them when was in school—they're very slow, very dreary—furthermore, the people that make them think that in order to be educated, you have to do it with words. So they have this horrible narrator, with his voice droning away, only it's a deep, cultured voice droning away—they are not showing it with pictures. It's just a boring monologue. Now the kids just turn their ears off, because who wants to listen to that. You can read it in a book.

Another fault of the older educational films is that the cuts are interminably long. They spent a lot of money to get all this footage, and why waste it? You've got to put it all in—particularly when cameramen do the cuts themselves—they like to leave in every golden frame.

Another problem is that an awful lot of educational films I've seen go so far as to have a classroom scene in which there will be a bunch of little kids—all sitting very straight, their legs crossed primly—none of them assuming casual, normal positions that real students would—and they're all gazing with rapt attention at this guy up at the front of the class, who is telling things and drawing diagrams on the board—that makes it visual.

An educational film does not have to simulate a classroom to be educational. As a matter of fact, that turns the kids off. They're looking forward to seeing a film because it's a day of freedom for them. The poor teachers have to watch these dreary things year after year, and they get pretty sick of it.

The current generation that is going to be watching these films—ever since they have been crawling around on the floor, there has been a television set around the house—has a very strong visual orientation, and particularly now since the television nowadays is getting more and more strongly visual. I've found in films of mine that they can see a frame, but you have to have black behind it to allow the persistence of vision to carry it on. But their minds are taking in a lot more—they're capable of perceiving quicker things, faster things—and furthermore, they're used to a little more in the way of color excitement, again because of television. Hollywood films are finally picking it up. They're always about 10 years behind the times. *Deep Blue World* is for those keen young minds, educational, but not boring."

117

THE WORLD OF KINESTASIS by Charles Braverman

How to Make Your Own Complete Color Sound
Movie About Anything For Less Than $50.00!

A student filmmaker, or an entire class, can
make a film on just about any subject in the
world without leaving the classroom! It may
sound impossible, but you can do it by using
the technique of "kinestasis."

American Time Capsule is probably the best
example for the beginner because in that film
I used only still photographs, cut to a sound
track of a drum solo by Sandy Nelson. *World
of '68* used live-action film clips in addition to
stills, which may be a bit tricky for the first try.
Nevertheless, it is a technique you might want
to use in a later kinestasis film.

The process may look complicated, but it is very
simple and can be lots of fun to work with. Ide-
ally, you would use a 16mm camera that can
shoot one frame at a time, a tripod, a music
stand or easel to hold the photos, two photo-
flood lamps, and the proper type of indoor color
film. If you do not have a 16mm camera, you
can use a Super-8 camera (preferably one with
a zoom lens, like the Bolex Macro-Zoom). You
will have to experiment with the Super-8 to determine how light a touch will give you a one
or two frame exposure. The reason for this is
that you will want to match your film, as much
as is possible, with the musical sound track.

Next, pick a suitable subject for your film. One
that you can develop with plenty of photographs
or paintings from books and other sources. Some
topics might be history, sports, travel, your
home town, or your school activites. Once you
have a good selection of pictures, you should
arrange them in the sequence that you want,
deciding shots that you want to emphasize, and
those that you want to treat quickly. As you
shoot the film, you will want a rhythmic pattern.
You may want to repeat some shots for emphasis. The still photos can also be animated when
you slowly pan across a photo or use your lens
to zoom "in" on a particular face or object in
the next photo.

Your next task is to pick a good sound track for
the film. One with a distinct beat that will give
you direction for shooting. The simplest way to
photograph the film to the sound track is to
transfer the music you want to use to a tape.
The end result can be shown by screening the
film to taped music, although precision cutting
to the music will be difficult. The approximate
matching of sound to music will yield a cruder
result than more sophisticated lab techniques,
but it can be fun anyway. It would be better,
if possible, to use a camera with a single frame
release, which some Super-8 cameras have.

Set up your shooting schedule, organize your equipment, and have your pictures in order. Set up the camera on a tripod in front of the picture stand, with the floodlights aimed at the pictures but not causing a glare. Be sure you shoot the pictures in sequence. This eliminates editing the film, gives you a one-to-one shooting ratio, and you can't ask for a better situation than this. Using your light touch for the shots (remember, you have experimented with the camera and know pretty well how many frames are shot by feel), you can proceed. Two-frame shots are very fast, about as short as you want them. Seven-to ten-frame shots obviously give a quick, but more fixed image. By knowing what to emphasize, and through a close acquaintance with the sound track, you can determine the length of each exposure. You can play around with visual rhythm in length of shots to the music and get some interesting effects.

When you have shot your Super-8 film, send it out for developing and show it, when it returns, to the tape-recorded music. If you have been careful about timing, it should work and you should have an exciting film.

For those who want to make a more sophisticated and accurate film in 16mm, single-frame form, you should use a 16mm reflex camera, with a zoom lens and a shutter release capable of exposing only one frame at a time. A Bolex Rex or Beaulieu are perfect and can usually be

rented from most good camera stores for prices ranging from $5.00 to $15.00 a day. You may not be able to focus as close as you wish with the zoom lens. This can be easily corrected by renting, for $.50 or so, "plus diopter" lenses that fit the front of the zoom lens. With these you can get as close as a few inches and still be in sharp focus.

For an accurate film, choose an appropriate musical sound track. Send it to a film-sound studio for transfer on to a 1/4-inch tape (7-1/2 inches per second). Edit it to a shorter length if you desire. Give the studio precise instructions about the sound track when you send it to them to make a positive and negative optical track on 16mm film (which should cost about $10.00 each, depending on the length). An optical track is simply sound made visible on film.

When you receive the transfers back, put the negative track away in a safe place. Your actual sound track on the finished print will be made from this. The negative track is all black, except for the optical sound track area. The positive track is all clear film except for the optical track

rea. Make sure you are working with both op-
ical tracks heads out. This means you won't
be working with your sound running backwards.
Be sure that you instruct the sound lab to mark
the film as to which end is *heads* and which
s *tails*.

By looking at the positive optical track, you
will see that it is a line that goes up and down.
Every time the line goes up, a sound was made
on the track. The more it goes up, the louder
the sound is. The rhythmic pattern is visible
to guide you in cutting.

f you want your pictures to be timed out to
music, count the number of frames (perforation
holes in the film) between the large escalations
shown on the optical track line. You will have
the total length of your film counted in frames
between beats corresponding to the musical
sound.

Remember to set your camera on single-frame
exposures, and then shoot one frame at a time,
guided by your frame count sheet. Remember
that you won't want to give a picture less than
a two-frame exposure. Your range might be from
two to 12 frames varying according to your sense
of visual rhythm corresponding with the music,
and your emphasis in the sequences.

Once you have shot the 16mm film, send it to
be developed. When you receive it from the
lab, do not project it! This can cause scratches
on the final print. There is one more step before
you have the completed sound, color film. Send

the original film back to the lab with the negative optical track you have been saving. Instruct
the lab to make a composite print, synchroniz-
ing the first frame of the picture with the first
frame of sound.

If all went well and you followed instructions,
you should get back a fast-moving, original,
sound color movie at very little cost. It will be
your creation, and it should give you an exhila-
rating sense of fulfillment.

There are more advanced techniques of making
kinestasis films that involve animation stands,
field guides, color filters, cells, cut-outs, and
live-action clips. You should probably begin simply and use more advanced techniques as you
become comfortable with the process. Those
I have described will work, and you will probably
be amazed at the results if you are careful with
your production work and think out your film
well. Good luck! Now make your film.

121

Reprinted from *MEDIA & METHODS, November, 1969*

CONCLUSION:

It is difficult to assess the future role of the kinestasis technique. Certainly it is unlikely that viewers will soon see a feature film completely photographed through kinestasis. Ninety minutes of kinestasis would amount to about 108,000 images, which would probably blow the eyeballs of the viewer right out of his head. There will, however, be variations on the technique incorporated into feature films and documentaries, using cuts at varying speeds to illustrate a process, a transitional sequence in time, or aspects of an object or a person. When the zoom lens appeared, it seemed that some features were a zoom-zoom dance, but that quieted down and the technique is now used with restraint. Kinestasis will probably assume its proper role in the language of the film and add to its dimensions.

The exciting aspect of kinestasis is that it does show the thrill of discovery that a new medium-like film can offer. Unlike changes in the grammar of language, we can more easily observe the rapidly changing grammar of the film because it is visual. Students can have a lot of fun using the technique, and watching films like these will enliven a classroom setting. The acceptance of kinestasis also reflects changes in the perceptions of people. Sylvia Dees pointed out that Hollywood used to feel that no cut should be less than 48 frames long. Rules in the film world, however, fall quickly. We now know that people can perceive and respond to ranges of cuts from two to eight frames in a continuous context. Commercials use the kinestasis technique liberally. In fact, to stay on the Dew-line of film language, one should watch commercials carefully. Advertising agencies have the talent and the money to experiment.

"Life is always worth living, if one has such responsive sensibilities. But we of the highly educated classes (so-called) have most of us got far, far away from Nature. We are trained to seek the choice, the rare, the exquisite exclusively, and to overlook the common. We are stuffed with abstract conceptions and glib with verbalities and verbosities; and in the culture of these higher functions the peculiar sources of joy connected with our simpler functions often dry up, and we grow stone-blind and insensible to life's more elementary and general goods and joys.'

—William James,
"On a Certain Blindness in Human Beings"

"What shall be grand in thee must needs be plucked at from the skies, and dived for in the deep, and featured in the unbodied air."

—Herman Melville

124

MOODS OF SURFING

KY CAPERS

CATCH THE JOY—DUNE BUGGIES

SKI THE OUTER LIMITS

TURNED ON

FULL FATHOM FIVE

He goes alone to meet the sea on its own terms:
Fugitive from the familiar hostile land,
seeking an extension into the beyond,
a better perspective to gauge his fears,
his worth, his finite kinesthetics.
He goes to watch the puppets on the shoreline
from the eye of something greater.

. . . The surfer, more animal than he knows,
is animal by situation.
He falls through the forest of air to water

The beasts of waves slouch low and alive,
rise angrily against the land and die.
The hunter-animal, who would die on land—
who would die at sea—
finds his life on this bleeding margin.
The battleground of peace,
where the animal-man-surfer draws life
from the rough beasts of the sea.

Alone enough to care and know,
the animal surfer seeks out his kind:
the roughhewn cuts of the sea
that defy the crazed stupidities of transistorized
    man.
The animal surfer is a higher form of life:
he makes his nest among the acts of god.

—From, "The Surfer, The Land and The Sea"
by Drew Kampion, *SURFER magazine, September,*
1969, pp. 94-95

MOODS OF SURFING

film by Greg MacGillivray and Jim Freeman.

oni Silver Medal—Cortina, Italy.
old Medal Award—International
ilm Festival of New York. Golden
agle Award—CINE, Washington,
.C. Chris Statuette—Columbus
ilm Festival. Award of Merit—
anders Film Reviews. Best Film
ward—Photographic Society of
merica. Cindy Award—Information
ilm Producers Association.

ime: 15 min.; Color

istributed by Pyramid

Moods of Surfing is a skillfully edited series of sequences taken from a 90-minute feature film called *Free and Easy* that MacGillivray and Freeman have shown to surfing enthusiasts throughout the world. It is a lyrical visual poem, presented without dialogue and with a musical score that fits each mood. Stunning colors, the poetry of motion, and the theme of man challenging the power and force of the sea involves the viewer and leaves him with a new sense of awareness. It is a very sensory film, emphasizing the kinetic, the tactile, and the visual.

THE FILM:

Regarding the structure of the film, Jim Freeman said:

"It starts out with a definite mood—an artistic approach trying to give a point of view. It shows what it's like to be near a surfboard, as a fish might see it from the water. From there it goes into a sunset, a late afternoon feeling with the seagulls landing and the surfers surfing. This is the opening sequence. It sets a unique mood—something you only experience five or 10 minutes before sunset.

From there, the film establishes larger waves—and the fun involved in surfing. Then it goes into comedy, the crowded aspect of surfing on smaller waves which is like a Friday afternoon on the Hollywood Freeway. There is always one determined person who wants to get through the whole mess, even though he's supposed to wait in line. Somehow he bops and trips over people's boards and heads and rear ends. Then we see a body surfing at the Wedge (at Newport Beach, California). If you have a low budget and a low I.Q., try surfing at the Wedge. It's a unique situation. You travel from deep to shallow water, with a little jetty in the way and an interesting wave that peels off the jetty. All it takes is sheer determination to ride the Wedge—that's all you need. The picture speaks for itself.

From there, the film moves over to the biggest waves in the world, at Waimea Bay, Hawaii. After that, it closes with the ballet surfer David Nuuhiwa.

Is there a theme? I think it goes back to the title —it shows the many moods of surfing. The average person looks at surfing as one ride on one wave. What we've attempted to do here is show him that there are many different types of rides and many different types of waves. We tried to complement this with various photographic techniques . . . It goes back to one word—variety.

The mature surfer is a well-rounded individual, and he looks at surfing as a completely separate thing from anything else in his life. He has a chance to divorce himself from society, work, school, whatever it may be and go out to the ocean and become completely engulfed in nature. Yet he's not becoming a slave—he's becoming a master. He's trying to go out there and harness a little bit of nature's energy. He comes back to his regular role in life when he's through. It's a combined effort of God and man. I think that's what surfing really is. You are harnessing part of God and you are sharing as well. It is a 50-50 thing. The bigger the wave, of course, the more you are sharing.

I think the most beautiful thing in surfing is the solitude—not to mention the physical benefits. Surfing requires a lot of physical strength, and it helps to keep you in excellent physical condition. It's a beautiful sport."

To read *Moods of Surfing* is to realize the care, the taste, and the courage that went into making the film. It's a film that inevitably "stokes" people (a surfing term equivalent to "reacting with great enthusiasm"). It is gorgeous, exciting, and poetic, as well as humorous.

AFTER THE FILM:

1. Discuss the different moods you found in the film.
2. Can you write "action images" or verbs which vividly describe the motion in the film?
3. From simply viewing the film how do you experience the events in the film—your encounters with the waves?
4. Could you write or film other motion sports where your senses come alive, such as motorcycle riding, sailing, or swimming?
5. Read about the sea. What images come to mind?
6. What are the satisfactions of surfing? Why is it so popular?

HOW *MOODS OF SURFING* WAS MADE:

Jim Freeman remarked that:

"We tried to approach the variety of all the moods of the surfer through different media of photography—through filters, slow motion, helicopters, etc. This is the first surfing film to use a lot of water shots, which are really subjective. Water shots involve placing the camera in a waterproof plexiglass housing. The cameraman is out in the water where surfers ride past the camera. It gives a very stunning effect. We usually film it in slow motion at 64 frames per second.

That way the movement is dramatized and amplified. At 24 frames per second which is the standard speed, the surfer would just go by in a flash. Slow motion makes it very poetic; you see water droplets that look like diamonds, and the wave actually takes on a shape as it progresses.

Many people are not aware that the film is shot in slow motion. Our feeling is that if people don't know about it, it's just fine. We think that shooting it in slow motion makes it more of a fantasy . . . and it certainly amplifies that one moment just a little bit longer.

Ninety-five percent of *Moods of Surfing* was shot with two cameras, so every ride has two angles. When we see the best angles sometimes we intercut with the water camera, back up with the land camera, so there will be two or three cuts on that one ride. But most of the time, we use 300 to 400mm telephoto lenses. Hollywood doesn't even use lenses this long because they are afraid there will be vibrations, or that they can't pan smoothly enough. We perfected our own tripod heads, which have heavy duty fluid similar to 100 weight grease. No matter how hard we try to turn it or pan with it, the head offers resistance. So, even if there's quite a bit of wind the pans will be completely smooth. Long lenses present an interesting angle, but the perspective remains very static. This is why we employ the water camera, which again changes the point of view completely. If you get tired of those two angles, you can always use the helicopter. The effect is interesting because you look down as well as alongside the surfer. Sometimes we mounted cameras on surfboards.

129

This is nice for an intercut, but it isn't good as a steady diet, because the horizon tilts with the surfboard. Some kind of a gyro would help. We've worked on this, but without much success. It's too delicate. And the surfer with the camera has a tendency to be more for himself and the wave than he is for the camera and the equipment. If we could find a good cameraman who was also a good surfer, I think we could keep the horizon steady.

The principal location of *Moods of Surfing* was the island of Oahu, Hawaii. Most of the shots were filmed on the north shore, which is about 45 minutes from Waikiki and includes Sunset Beach, Waimea Bay, with the largest waves in the world. These giant swells travel from as far away as Alaska, and are almost unnoticed, because the water is so deep. They're traveling along at 30 or 40 mph. and all of a sudden BAM —they hit these shallow reefs off the island of Oahu. The rolling swell suddenly becomes a giant wave, because of this shallow reef in Waimea Bay. The reef, combined with the off-shore trade winds which are common in Hawaii, help to hold the wave up.

The comedy or human interest sequence was filmed at Malibu, California. We chose Malibu because it is the most crowded beach. Everyone goes there to learn how to surf. You find good surfers as well as novices. It's very interesting the way the two combine and tangle and get shoved off their boards. You see that in the film.

All the major surfers in the film are experts, surfing for at least eight years. They make their living, in one way or another, off surfing, either through endorsing boards or modelling. The main fellow who comes to mind is David Nuuhiwa, often called the ballet dancer of surfing. His sequence closes *Moods of Surfing.* The other individuals star in one or two rides, whereas David Nuuhiwa stars in eight or nine rides.

The beginning sequence up to the title was exclusively shot in the water in slow motion— 64 frames per second. The surfing you see in this sequence is called getting inside the tube. The surfer is riding the most critical part of the wave the longest amount of time. I guess this can be equated with a skier on a ski jump, or a sky-diver in a free fall. It is what every surfer is searching for—to be in the tube, and to do it very gracefully. We tried to show it as an art form, using good light and slow motion to make it more or less romantic. It's an average thing that these surfers do quite frequently, but we dramatized it through technique.

's in natural color. We don't like to use filters
nless perhaps in an artificial dreamlike se-
uence. We are firm believers in using available
ght, and our formula is very simple. We only
hoot when the sun is out—never on an over-
ast day, and we play with the sun. We always
et our most dramatic shots after it has rained,
hen the sky is free of haze and, generally
peaking, we have a pencil-blue horizon.

o get dramatic effect, we try to place the sun
ehind the surfer so he's backlit. We get enough
ll from the white water to make the front of
e surfer's face light up so he's not a silhou-
tte. We consider this to be one of our greater
chievements in the film—to backlight the
urfer, yet still have definition. You get twinkles
n the water, which is very artistic for enhancing
e slow motion—a totally involved feeling which
e David Nuuhiwa sequence, especially, por-
ayed.

here were quite a few problems in the film-
ng. The most amusing—it seems amusing now,
ut at the time it wasn't—was when my partner,
reg, was out in the water at Sunset Beach. He
as sitting on a surfboard with his waterproof
amera. You shoot in a channel. The waves break
ver a reef, and of course, you don't sit on the
eef, because you'd naturally get swept up and
go over the falls" or into the breaking wave.
o he was shooting in the channel, photograph-
ng these surfers, and he became so engrossed
n his photography that he wasn't aware that
e peak at Sunset was shifting, and where he
as filming was the channel, but it soon became

the wave. It has a tendency to do this in Hawaii,
with the tremendous currents and the tremendous amount of force that's in those waves. It
changes from a north swell to a northwest swell.
The swell changed on him and he didn't realize
it, but he was right in the middle of the breaking wave, and he went over the falls with the
camera and the board. We never did find the
camera, the board washed in about two hours
later, and Greg had his lights knocked out for
a few seconds. That's about the closest to losing
a cameraman that we've come, to say nothing of
a partner and a friend. We lost the camera, of
course, and those are the best shots we've ever
taken. We'll always say that because they got
away.

The worst part about it was I was filming the
whole thing on shore, and there wasn't one little
thing I could do about it except focus a little
harder on the giant telephoto lens and watch the
petrified expression on his face, but it all happened so quickly, you couldn't tell, really—just
pray a little.

A few winters ago, we used a helicopter to shoot several of the sequences. The helicopter pilot is a very good friend of mine, and he has a tendency to try to please the photographer, maybe just a little too much. He has a tendency to forget he's a helicopter pilot, and not a surfing-photographer-pleaser. In this one instance, we came in so low, and I was demanding and shouting and screaming through the headphones that run between the pilot and myself. I was screaming to go down and down and down and we were actually parallel as well as in the line of sight of the surfer. I could look right out and touch his hand as well as see the expression on his face. Then, I looked up and saw this wave feathering overhead, and it got to the point—either blow the shot or get wet. So, as we started to pull up, the wave touched the skids on the helicopter and got the bottom of my feet wet, because I was hanging out the door. I had myself strapped in, but I had my feet hanging out so I could get a better angle. The helicopter people didn't care for getting salt water all over the engine.

The other thing that was interesting was filming up high, as we like to do, looking down at the surfer from the helicopter, presenting a unique angle where we can study his footwork on the larger waves. As the wave breaks, you get a tremendous suction downward, because of the offshore breeze. To make a long story short, your helicopter becomes very similar to a Ping-Pong ball at Niagara Falls—there's only one way to go, and that's down.

This particular time, we got sucked down with the wave—we lost our air. As most people know, the helicopter actually creates air by hitting it off the ground, and it bounces back up. The helicopter has to have air to chew to keep it up. When the air is all sucked down, there's no air for it to chew, and consequently it has to go down with the downdraft. We hit the water with our pontoons. Finally, enough air came back and it sucked us back up, and just at that time, the wave came in and it was pretty close. We risked a helicopter for those pictures, not to mention the camera, cameraman, and pilot.

There were no serious injuries at all in filming *Moods of Surfing*. The biggest problem in surfing isn't really you or your surfboard—it's someone else's surfboard. Someone else loses his surfboard, and it becomes like a car out of control. This can be very dangerous because a

wave picks it up and bounces it around like a cork and it can hit you in the head. It has happened to several people, but fortunately it's just been a bruise instead of a bump in the head, which could cause a concussion or a black-out, or even death.

To my knowledge, no one was killed when we filmed this. Surfing is one of the safest sports around. In fact, more people are killed falling off step-ladders every year than by surfing. There are almost one million surfers in the world today. But, since we've been filming surfing, there have been fewer than 20 deaths. That's a pretty good ratio, especially considering how much time each surfer spends participating in the sport.

That big wave sequence is very scary. Slow motion dramatizes it. It takes a lot of courage to surf those big waves. You have to be in top physical condition too. You have to be able to hypo-ventilate—take a series of deep breaths before you take off. You hold your breath as you're going down the face of each wave, hoping and praying the wave doesn't collapse on you, but nine times out of 10, it does collapse on you, or the whole Pacific Ocean comes in on you. Then you have to hold your breath for 15 or 20 seconds—it seems more like 15 or 20 hours.

the course of being held under the water,
here's such a tremendous force, you sometimes
change directions and you think up is down and
you even hit the bottom—occasionally get
bounced off the bottom, and by the time you
realize up is up, you're almost out of the air,
and this is 20 or 30 seconds later, and that's
a long, long, time to be under.

We shot more than 100,000 ft. of film. To watch
it uncut would take 50 continuous hours. It took
us a year and a half to produce the film. The
cutting alone took four months. But remember,
Free and Easy is a 90-minute film. *Moods of
Surfing* was an offshoot, and didn't take long
to make. The sound track is library music, which
is usually against you to begin with. Good library
music is hard to find. I went down and played
records for three days, and came up with seven
or eight songs. We concentrated on a theme
song which opens and closes *Moods of Surfing.*
It's called "Distant Dreams" on a Martin label—
it's only on 78's, and you have to buy it from
the library. It never was released on a 33-1/3
or a popular disc. Ironically, it was considered
not good enough for public consumption, so it
ended up in the library. It's a nice song and fits
the movie very well. The other music was intended to enhance the moods of the scenes.

We ended up cutting the film to the music. We
picked up this music and we were unhappy with
the way it laid in—it just didn't happen to fall
into place—so we juggled the sequences around
so that some of the high notes would punctuate
the surfing shots and the crescendo would be
with finishing a ride or something of this nature.

The comedy sequence was cut to music also,
so that it's very well punctuated when a guy
falls off his board or some other action takes
place.

I'm very happy the music worked out as well
as it did. An original score would probably be
better, but you're talking a lot more money and
there's a big risk that you might not end up with
anything. With library music you can hear what
you have when you start, and you can have a
definite direction.

For us, *Moods of Surfing* expresses the essence
of what we think is the most exciting free sport
in the world."

137

SKY CAPERS

A film produced by David Adams.
Filmed by Carl Boenish. Edited
by Fred Hudson.

Original sound track by Michael
Curb

Award of Merit—Columbia
International Film Festival.
President of the Republic Award—
CIDALC, Grenoble '70 Film Festival
Time: 15 min.; Color

Distributed by Pyramid

Sky Capers is about the thrills and spills of sky-diving. Over a period of four years, sky-diving enthusiast and filmmaker Carl Boenish photographed many aspects of the sport, using helmet-mounted cameras controlled by wire attachments to the diver's hand. Doing most of his filming at Lake Elsinore, Calif., he got about 8,000 ft. of film, which Fred Hudson edited down to an exciting 15 minutes that catch the perils and exhilaration of the sport. The film was purchased by United Artists and played in theaters with the Beatles' film, *Yellow Submarine*.

THE FILM:

In the opening shot, sky-divers plunge from a plane to the accompaniment of the sound of howling wind. As the titles come on, we hear the rock song, "Fly High," which is the theme of the film. Then the film cuts to para-sailing in which a parachutist is pulled along the ground or water until he rises high into the air. Then we experience free-fall shots from various angles—from within the plane, from under the parachutist—and from above him. The daring of one diver is shown as he falls, without helmet or shoes, with the pack on his back. One sky-diver releases his reserve chute—a multitude of oranges.

In the middle of the film, there is a comedy sequence of speeded-action, which creates a feeling of old-time Chaplinesque caricature. Sky-divers march. They hit the ground with extreme speed, one landing in the lake and squishing his way through the mud. The plane sounds like a wound-up toy.

The stunning final sequences show the difficult "star formation" in which groups of sky-divers join hands in the air. At one point, there are eight in one formation. They look like bugs from outer space, joining in the air as they are silhouetted against the sky. The final shot of striking beauty is of a diver descending at night, with the moon in the background.

The titles of the film are achieved by optical printing. The credits at the end are rendered through optical multiple-image processes—a snappy conclusion to a film that is unusual, both in subject matter and cinematographic technique.

AFTER THE FILM:

1. Describe your feelings as if you were one of the sky-divers. How would it feel to plummet through space in a free-fall?
2. What were the most effective shots in the film?
3. What, for you, was unusual about the film? If you were to make a film like it, what techniques would you use?
4. How does this film illustrate the lengths to which a filmmaker must go for his art?
5. Compare the film *The Gypsy Moths* with *Sky Capers.* Carl Boenish filmed the free-fall segments of both films.
6. Do you know of any poetry about the sky?

HOW *SKY CAPERS* WAS MADE:

Sky-divers leave the plane at a high altitude and have remarkable powers of manipulation in the air. In a free-fall, they can somersault, control turns, and vary the rate of descent to join other divers in star formations. Their rate of descent is from 120 to 160 mph. Shooting much of the film in slow motion, makes them appear to fall more slowly.

When the diver's altimeter indicates 2500 ft., he must open his chute, trying to land on target. Smoke attachments on feet or hands mark his descent for those on the ground.

The musical sound track and lyrics are by Michael Curb and Michael Lloyd. The words are sung by the California Spectrum. Michael Curb also composed the music for *Skater Dater.*

Fred Hudson, who edited *Sky Capers* and did some of the pick-up shots for it, made the following comments:

"A basic decision was that we should make a 15-to 20-minute film to meet the needs of libraries and theaters.

There is a progression in the film from simple to complex. A simple air maneuver is the parasailing—shot on the Riviera, I think—in which they pull this guy into the air. This is contrasted with the rather complex free-falling in the air, where a chute has to be used to keep from slamming into the earth. Basically, it's just a man cavorting free in the air, using gymnastics and intricate maneuvers that were unheard of 10 or 15 years ago.

It turned out, after screening all this footage, that there were some big masses of people in the air doing complicated things. We felt this was the ace-in-the-hole—the main thing we should build towards. We started to find other things that would help the film evolve towards this climax.

As exciting as sky-diving might be to watch, there wasn't enough material to carry it for 18 minutes. It has to move right along in the theater. The idea was to have some comic relief. There were some shots that might have aroused a giggle. But again, what do you do with it? How do you build a sequence that may be a minute long? Do you show a series of pratfalls, or what?

I got some stuff isolated, but there was never quite enough. Then I happened upon this thing of cheating with optical printing. We exaggerate —some things that aren't quite funny in a normal speed become funny by increasing the speed by two or three times. Where a guy comes down in a chute, he lands and runs away—it's kind of funny. At double or triple the speed it becomes a caricature.

So we settled on that technique. Then we tried to tangle them all together to be a sequence by editing these funny little pratfalls, and it seemed to work. Then we stuffed it into the picture. In isolation, it was kind of funny, but in the picture, it didn't seem to fit. It came in too suddenly, so we had to work very hard to find a way to get into the sequence. We found a solution which never was really great, but it seemed to work.

That was a very difficult thing to do. It's one of the hardest things I've done in editing, and yet it doesn't look like an awful lot. But the scenes were all made. They were all manhandled from the original material. The original material and the final result are very different.

All the free-fall stuff was shot with cameras on the helmets. The camera held 50 ft. of film in a magazine. The control was through a wire to the arm. The cameraman had a type of eye-piece. As he's free-falling, he looks through this eye-piece that is held stationary by the helmet. Once he has the guy sighted, he can start filming.

Carl Boenish has since filmed the free-fall sequences in *The Gypsy Moths.* Now he looks at *Sky Capers* as very amateurish, but it gets a great response from audiences."

ABOUT CARL BOENISH:

In the summer of 1962, a challenge from a friend prompted Carl Boenish to make his first parachute jump. Since then, he has made 941 jumps. He has been filming on the way down in about 700 of them. All in all, he has spent a total of about 12 hours doing free-falls. The accumulated time spent riding in an open parachute would add up to almost two days.

After Carl Boenish had made about 100 jumps, he became intrigued with various aspects of filming while free-falling. The state of the art was in its infancy then, and only two or three people in the country were filming while falling. In 1964, Carl Boenish was the first known sport parachutist to mount a camera in the lines of a parachute before it opened.

Carl has supplied the free-fall footage for nine different films, including television documentaries, the ABC Wide World of Sports, a film for the United States Parachute Association, and two feature-length films, both produced at the MGM studios.

His first movies were made with a hand-held 8mm camera. He next used a helmet-mounted 16mm camera and now uses a 12 pound 35mm camera mounted on his helmet. "Shooting in wide-screen format for features," he says, "is a real challenge, resulting in some very exciting footage."

Carl started jumping just after he turned 21 years old. He was graduated from the University of Southern California at 23 with a degree in electrical engineering. He worked for four years with the Hughes Aircraft Company, specializing in radar and laser electronics. His interest in film-making and parachuting increased to the point where he presently devotes his full-time work to parachuting and shooting.

Regarding sky-diving, Carl remembers the time when a six-man star was the world's record. In 1967, he filmed the new world's record at the time—a 10-man star. He has also filmed the female world record, an eight-girl star.

Carl has made scores of exhibition jumps, including jumping at various military installations, Lynwood City Park, the Great Western Exhibit (100 yards from the Santa Ana Freeway), into the ocean, night jumping (both on land and into the water), and high altitude jumping (up to 30,000 ft., using an oxygen mask).

Carl Boenish described one of the most important jumps of his life. "Three of us were helping a local theater premiere the movie, *The Gypsy Moths,* which took us almost a year to film. We received permission from the FAA, the State of California, the police and fire departments, the board of supervisors, land owners, and a myriad of other people, and we pulled off flawlessly the jump of all jumps up to now. From 3,000 ft. at night, the three of us jumped into the parking lot of the theater, near the corner of Sunset and Vine in the heart of Hollywood. We had strobe lights and flares, and all of us made stand-up landings near the target, right in the middle of a large crowd and a parade. That jump will live for a very long time to come."

143

CATCH THE JOY—DUNE BUGGIES

A film by Greg MacGillivray and Jim
Freeman.

Time: 15 min.; Color

Distributed by Pyramid

"He who kisses the joy as it flies
Lives in eternity's sunrise"

—William Blake

Another new sport is riding the dunes in a dune
buggy. Jim Freeman spent three months at the
Pismo Dunes in California, where this sport is
the rage. In the section on how the film was
made, he describes some of the problems he
encountered while trying to catch the dynamic
spirit of the sport, the competition, and the
beauty of the buggies in action.

THE FILM:

The picture begins with a striking shot that shows
a puzzling design, somewhat like meringue on a
pie with a ladybug on top. As the camera slowly
zooms in, we see that these riffles are actually
the dunes, and the ladybug is another sort of
bug called a dune buggy. Then we hear the mo-
tor rev up and the competition begins. The buggies charge up the dunes. Some make it. Some
don't. We also see motorcycles trying the course.
From the competition, we turn to thrilling shots
of buggies whirling around the dunes, literally
flying over some of them, sometimes skidding
very close to the camera.

Then we experience a sequence of a boy and a
girl riding over the dunes, ending with a com-
parative shot of the buggy riding along the sea,
the waves of dunes on one side, the waves of
the ocean on the other.

Next we see sand skiing and sand surfing with
boards. Then there is a wild ride on a flat metal
sled attached to the buggy. The beauty of motion
and speed, plus humor is caught in these sequences.

As the sun sets, we see silhouette shots of the
buggy against the sun and the moment of sunset on the sand.

AFTER THE FILM:

1. How does this sport compare with auto-rac-
   ing?
2. Could you write a first-person account of a
   ride on a dune buggy?
3. Car enthusiasts may wish to look into the
   history of the automobile and all the variations of the machine that now exist.
4. Compare a film on racing, such as *Grand Prix*
   or *Winning* with this film. How do they differ
   in effect and content? How are they similar?
5. Both *Dunes* and *Catch The Joy* were shot at
   the Pismo Dunes. Show both films and compare and contrast them as to intent, the style
   of the photographers and editors, and the
   total effects of both.
6. Compare and contrast *The Moods of Surfing*
   with *Catch The Joy*. What similarities do you
   find between the films as to shots, effects,
   and feelings of the people? What are the dif-
   ferences?

HOW *CATCH THE JOY* WAS MADE:

Jim Freeman shot 30,000 ft. of film to make this picture. He said:

"The idea has been in the back of my mind for about seven years. In fact, before I began surfing movies, I had a giant curiosity for these sand dunes. I remember seeing them in Death Valley when I was a little boy and then I spent a lot of time up in Pismo Beach with some relatives. It used to fascinate me, seeing these old Model T's or old-time cars just completely stripped with wide tires. They'd actually split rims and weld them together, and then they'd put a regular tire on them which would make them oversized because of the wide rim. I thought it was marvelous how these vehicles would be putting around in the sand dunes defying nature because normally sand is instant death for a car. You lose traction.

Over the years, my photographic ability increased, and somehow, the dune buggies increased and the engines became bigger—they had 427 cu. in. and over 400 hp. They looked like miniature dragsters. Several of my friends became interested in the dune buggy sport and it was almost a natural to go out and watch them. There was so much poetic involvement—so many beautiful things with this vast array of sand dunes, the loneliness, and one little speck of buggy and one little speck of man out there. The buggy looked like an intruder, yet somehow it conquered the dunes because it could go anyplace.

In the film we tried to capture the many moods of the sand dunes. We filmed all this in the late afternoon to provide low-key light with dramatic shadows to amplify the solitude, the loneliness of the dunes and the orange-patterned light you get at that time of day.

One particular section has a stretch that consists of just giant rolls. There are valleys and

little rolling mountains 30 or 40 ft. above. It looks like an ocean swell marching in towards shore. Only the dunes, of course, never break. They just keep rolling. It's very interesting to watch this buggy go from the valley, roll over the top and down again into the valley. It's very, very similar to surfing. A person paddling out at Waimea Bay or Sunset Beach has his heart in his throat because he just doesn't know exactly what is going to happen—whether the wave is going to break or not. In dune buggying there's just a beautiful feeling of up-and-down motion. The other thing that's really neat is to be able to take advantage of centrifugal force. You're able to go around a basin which is probably at a 75 or 80 deg. angle, and it's 360 deg. around, so you're actually going sideways around this face. The only way you can do it is to get up to a speed of 50 or 60 mph. If you stop, naturally you slide down and maybe even roll over, but by keeping up your speed, you stay against it.

It's not a dangerous sport. We've watched it for quite a few years. The only danger is the idiot behind the wheel. To overcome the problem they require you to wear a 13 ft. pole with a little flag on top. When I say wear, I mean the dune buggy carries it. You see this little flag on top, popping over a knoll before the dune buggy comes into view. This is the warning.

I think that dune buggying is every bit as safe as surfing, and probably a lot safer than skiing.

The average buggy is very simple to construct. If you want a functional machine, buy yourself a used, wrecked Volkswagen—one with a good engine and transmission. Pull off the body and all you have left is a frame. Most people like to shorten the frame. They take out about 18 in. in the center, so that the wheel base is shorter. They put a roll bar on it for safety's sake.

This can all be done for well under $600. If you have a slight ability to weld and a desire to build this thing, it's very interesting. If you don't care to go that route, you can spend a couple of thousand dollars and buy one, made by Myers Manx. It has a fiber glass body on a Volkswagen frame with the body cut down. It's licensed for the road, has a windshield, windshield wiper, brake lights, head lights, so it's completely safe for highway use as well as for sand dunes. This is very popular now.

The old school of thought was just to build a steel frame and put in a water-cooled Corvette engine. Nowadays, everyone is going toward the air-cooled engine, mainly because of the simplicity, but also because having the engine in the rear provides extra traction. Horsepower

is not the winning factor. The weight distribution and the wide tires with the little 36 hp. engine does amazing things out there."

FILMING *CATCH THE JOY:*

"Our biggest advantage in filming *Catch the Joy* was the natural beauty and drama of the dunes. To capture these qualities, we used a helicopter which gave us magnificent aerials. From several thousand feet, the dunes look like a Hollywood set—almost fake. In 10 seconds the helicopter drops from about 2,000 ft. down to about 10 in. This is to establish a dune buggy at the beginning of the picture. We see the aerial of the sand dunes, and we see a slight speck. This speck becomes a dot, and the dot soon turns into a giant dune buggy which fills the screen. This is our introduction.

We use the helicopter shots as a reference to show how minute this little man-made object is in the eyes of Nature. We also employed slow motion photography to dramatize sand flying off the buggies. And we used long lenses to give a compression feeling which again slows the pace down. We also took advantage of the fact that these beautiful sand dunes come down to the Pacific Ocean. It makes a nice combination— two beautiful things that Nature has to offer. Together, they create a sense of freedom.

Two of my friends are the stars of *Catch The Joy.* They were such good friends that they liked to help me get good shots. In fact, they liked to help so much that they wanted to see how close they could come to the camera without hitting it. The object was to get slow motion sand flying into the lens, not a fast motion dune buggy running over the lens. Occasionally, they'd get mixed up, and I was run over twice. When I say run over, I'm really exaggerating. My feet got run over, but the camera was completely demolished. Again, we saved the film, and that's all that really matters. The effect is startling—so was the camera bill. They're still my friends. They asked me if I wanted to do it one more time. That was usually my line after they'd gone off a cliff and dropped down 300 or 400 ft. I'd ask for another take because I'd like a different angle. This time, I thought the one shot—the one take—was just fine.

The biggest problem was the sand getting into the gate of the camera. A single grain of sand getting into the gate can cause a scratch which, magnified on the screen, looks like a telephone pole. We had to keep plastic bags around the film, and when we changed the film, we had to be very careful not to have even a grain of sand on our bodies that could get inside the camera.

Keeping the film out of the sun's heat was tricky. Another problem was that Pismo Beach is next to the Pacific Ocean and the fog bank often comes in just before sunset. We tried to have a late afternoon sunset feeling, and somehow Mother Nature wanted us to have a foggy feeling—so we spent three months up there, waiting for Mother Nature to change her mind.

We were there about 90 days and we shot about 45 mins. per day, because we wanted the dramatic shadows. We also had to wait for a wind to come along to erase any tracks because we wanted to get complete solitude—never show any tracks, people, litter, or anything that would bring you back to reality. In the one man alone sequence at the end of the film, if you notice carefully, there aren't any tracks, any buildings, any people—anything that shows man. We wanted to show strictly Mother Nature and the gentleman on the buggy.

We shot 30,000 ft. of film, which would run about 15 hours. It was fun to make the picture, in spite of the problems. It was a very rewarding experience. You learn to polish your patience—especially while you're waiting for a fog bank to disappear, or re-appear.

When we weren't shooting, we were repairing the dune buggies. They need minor adjustments, tune-ups and spot welds here and there, from a few jumps. The higher you get off the ground, the harder you come down, and every time you come down, you seem to break a weld.

Some of the stunts done in the film, I don't think the average dune buggy driver would want to try, because it was a hair on the dangerous side.

Like surfers, dune buggy people enjoy being out-of-doors, and in the sun. And their age can be anywhere from 6 to 60. Whereas, surfing fits the teenager and the 20-through about 25-year-old.

We cut our 15 hours of footage into a 15-min. film. It's a nice length. There is no narration, and we want our message to be told visually."

THE FILM:

"We divide it into five categories. We establish the buggy—then we go into sort of a competition sequence which shows what is done on a high competitive level with the dune buggies—how they can be modified to climb hills and drag race.

Then we go into a section with a boy and girl, showing how much fun they can have in the dune buggy. Then we have a little fun with a thing called the sand surfing board, which is a little 18-in. board with linoleum on the bottom. You put a little paraffin on it and it acts as a surfboard on the dunes. And there was this other fellow out there who thought he had a nice '46 Ford hood that served no purpose on the car. So we turned it upside down and attached it by a 100 ft. rope to the back of the dune buggy. We put a maniac who liked to crack the whip at the controls and the fellow on the hood said he could fry a couple of eggs on his rear end a couple of times. It was fun for him riding on the hood. It was fun for me to take pictures. Then the ending sequence goes back to showing the man alone on the sand dunes.

When you have an interesting subject, it can become monotonous after a few minutes. We've tried to present different moods through different camera techniques and then explore the mood and make it a fantasy. It's within reach, yet exaggerated to the point where it's not an everyday thing. It's kind of similar to *Moods of Surfing*. The score is a modern sound that the younger generation enjoys these days. It fits and punctuates the moods very nicely. Sound effects give a nice point of view and break up the wall-to-wall music feeling.

The film's main message is taken from William Blake's poem "Eternity." It's always been one of my favorite poems because of its everyday application and openness to interpretation—it can mean many different things to many different people. The poem fits well into what the film says, and I hope that our message of joy comes through."

149

SKI THE OUTER LIMITS

A film produced by Summit Films.

Double Awards—American Film Festival

Time: 27 min.; Color

Distributed by Pyramid

Ski the Outer Limits is the first film to win the EMILY AWARD, which is the top honor given to the film receiving the highest number of points in the American Film Festival. It contains some breath-taking, dazzling, spectacular sequences and some unusual photographic techniques, particularly the use of the high-speed camera.

Barry Corbet, one of the filmmakers who created the film, said about it:

"There have been so many ski films: trite, repetitive, pretty to watch at best. *Ski the Outer Limits* is different. By placing five of the world's finest skiers in controlled situations the film strives to equate man's search for involvement and meaning with the more graphic expression of the same quest reflected by the skiers."

The results are more than good. Quite often, they are fantastic.

THE FILM:

The opening sequence puts the viewer on skis, watching the snow and the spectacular scenery rush by. Then comes one of the film's great shots—a skier somersaulting forward off a cliff at Jackson Hole, dropping 60 ft., landing on his skis, and whizzing away. This shot and others that follow examine man testing the outer limits of his skill.

Sequences of professional contests, and young people learning the fundamentals of skiing, are relieved by comic episodes. A particularly amusing ballet sequence shows Bill Peterson performing to Enesco's music.

In slow motion, we experience the sensual feeling of skiing through powder snow. Near the end of the film, skiers somersault in slow motion over the camera. In the final sequence a middle-aged skier, racing down the slopes, still challenges the snow and tests the outer limits.

The total effect is one of exhilaration and appreciation of the lure of the sport.

AFTER THE FILM:

1. What do you think are the challenges and satisfactions of skiing?
2. How do you think the cameraman achieved some of the effects in the film?
3. Look at *Ski the Outer Limits* and *Moods of Surfing* one after the other. How do the films compare? How do they differ?
4. If you have first-hand experience of skiing—or you know someone who has—compare these experiences with what you saw in the film.
5. After seeing *Moods of Surfing, Sky Capers,* and *Ski the Outer Limits,* which of the sports the films describe would you choose?

HOW *SKI THE OUTER LIMITS* WAS MADE:

The film was shot over a period of five months in the United States and Europe. It was made for the Hart Ski Company, but the sponsor does not intrude upon the action, and allowed the film producers almost limitless freedom.

The shooting ratio of 20 to 1 resulted in a surfeit of material. This was the main problem in editing.

Five of the world's best skiers are the stars of the film. They are: Roger Staub (Olympic gold medalist), Arthur Furrer (best-known trick skier), Tom LeRoi (multiple front flippist), Hermann Gollner (multiple back flippist), and Bill Peterson (clown supreme). These men are filmed visiting beginning ski classes, high mountain glaciers, the European race circuit, deep powder field, and the outer space between take-off and landing.

There were problems. Gaining admission to major European ski races was not easy. A physical problem was the transportation of heavy camera equipment through glaciers and other hazardous terrain.

The producer feels that the most striking shot in the film is of Hermann Gollner doing a forward somersault at the Corbet Couloir at Jackson Hole. The sequence was filmed at the very high speed of 400 frames per sec., giving the effect of extreme slow motion on the screen.

From the producer's point of view, a highlight of the whole experience was the cameraman's solo descent—with a 16mm Arriflex, down the Argentiere glacier. They commented that the film crew as well as the skiers they photographed had to "press the outer limits" of skill and endurance.

TURNED ON

FULL FATHOM FIVE

Films produced by David Adams.
Both films edited by Ken Rudolph.

Bronze Medal Award—International
Film and TV Festival of New York.

Time: 8 min. (each film); Color

Distributed by Pyramid

Both films are superbly edited by Ken Rudolph.
Turned On is a fast-moving overview of action
sports such as surfing, skiing, snow-mobiling,
sailing, dune buggying and racing. The variety
and pace of the film in which one thrilling ep-
isode follows another just as thrilling, is a tri-
bute to the exciting photography—much of it
by Warren Miller—and the ingenious editing.

Full Fathom Five is an underwater film that captures the mystery and dream-like quality of life
beneath the sea. The inspired editing matches
the mood of the visual and the tempo of the
sound track with effect.

Crystals, which Ken Rudolph discusses at the
beginning of the following interview, is an abstract, beautiful film of crystals growing, photographed through the microscope by Herbert
Loebel.

THE ART OF EDITING:

An interview with Ken Rudolph:

"I had never attempted anything quite like
Crystals, cutting it just to music. It has always
been my favorite type of film. It all came to me
in a jumble. Apparently another cutter, or maybe
two cutters, had tried to work with it and failed.
They were trying to do it the normal way, but
I really find cutting to music better. It comes
out better if you're going to have just the sound
track with no narration. It's the natural way to
do it. That way, visuals and sound track are really
in league.

Also, as a cutter, I have a lot of freedom with
the music. If it's scored after it's cut, the editor
doesn't really fulfill his main function. The composer does at that point. But I feel that I understand my visuals better than the composer does.

Since it was the first film that I had done like
that, my biggest problem was with the music. I

have an absolute minimum of training in music.
I took several courses in college, but I don't
play an instrument, or haven't since I was a kid.
I'm a fantastic music fan and do understand it,
but I had never really worked with it. If I were
doing *Crystals* today, with the experience I have
had since then, the transitions would be far better. I think my attunement with the music would
be about the same, because I was pretty close
to that music. The music came to me in a jumble
too. I had more music than I had visuals. It was
a question of going through about 2,000 ft. of
magnetic film to come out with the frames I
wanted. That was quite a hassle.

They used polaroid filters with *Crystals.* They
vibrate, change colors. The one thing I didn't
like about *Crystals* was the fact that they only
used two background cuts, and not particularly
good colors, either. This made it very difficult
to get a color balance of the backgrounds. Hope-
fully, if I ever do anything like that again, I will
be able to tell the photographer a little more
of my needs.

In subsequent film, I edited the music first.
Turned On is totally edited out of music performed by Sandy Nelson on records. I cut in
and out of them at many opportunities. As a
matter of fact, I played a game. I thought I had
done such a good job that you couldn't tell. But
I played the dubbed score to a musician, and
he picked out every change. But still, it's pretty
darned good, I think.

I cut *Turned On* by the seat of my pants. I try
to invent techniques if I can. There are some
subtle things in it. *Full Fathom Five* is filled
with more things I've never seen before—more
so than *Turned On.* With *Turned On,* I believe
thoroughly in opposition of action-movement.
A strong cut should have continuity so that the
eye is not jarred. However, the action should
somehow change significantly.

I immerse myself in the music and get to know it so that I can hum the entire thing. And I really get in tune with the music and it says something to me visually. And I try, as best I can, to match the visuals to what it says. Again, the limitations are that I have a finite amount of footage. In *Turned On,* it was particularly finite. However, I would say my cutting ratio is still very high. Even in *Turned On,* it is probably at least 10 or 15 to one—of what I had to what I used. On *Full Fathom Five,* it was greater, and on the surfing film I'll be doing, it will be still greater. The more footage I have, the better off I am, even though it makes organizing more difficult. I am looking for a particular action that fits the mental pre-image so I have to have a great amount of footage.

Basically, I memorize the footage first. One of the reasons it takes me a long time to cut, and more than I feel that it should, is that I have to go through a memorization process. I have to know everything that I've got. When it's a matter of hundreds of shots that I have, it's not easy to get it all in my head.

I think *Turned On* is a very exciting film. There's no narration line. The cognitive processes of these films are what is called in the vernacular, "a trip," having nothing to do with the drug usage of trip, but then—it's very difficult to explain—I theorize to myself that I don't need a narrative line or any progression of images. The jumble is actually a good thing, because it takes you to different places. I think that particular kind of McLuhanistic cutting is becoming more common.

I learned a good lesson from the Braverman films that I organized—namely, the eye is able to do all sorts of beautiful things organizing images by itself, without the need for a cognitive, meaningful organization, as long as there's good continuity."

FULL FATHOM FIVE

"I really tried, at least in one portion, to do things that I'd never seen before, and honestly, until I see the opticals, I won't know what it really is going to look like. I have a picture in my head of what I hope it looks like. Because water is sort of amorphous, the music for that picture was very amorphous. It goes through a lot of changes, and a lot of different kinds of beats and modalities and stuff. I tried very hard to make the cutting correspond with the music, which means doing some very strange things — flashing images for just a second against a black background — off-cycle fade-in and fade-outs when it almost goes to black, but something comes and it sort of will look like it pulsates, if it works. Again, maybe I should do tests on these things, but I'm almost positive it will work — like 95 percent positive, and that's enough for me."

FILM ON FLOWERS

"I'm going to do a film on flowers which I expect will be my magnum opus. I've been sprouting creative wings. It's everything I've been building toward. Also, I will have had a chance to shoot, which I haven't had up to now. My training has been both as an editor and as a photographer. I may have had more experience as a photographer than as an editor. I miss it. I really would rather be photographing the films also. This way, I'll have a chance.

I've seen only about 15 percent of the footage, maybe not even that much, but I love it. It's colorful, and I respond very strongly to color. One sequence will be a wild series of dissolves — maybe four or five images on at the same time. I plan to make a lot of use of camera movement — mainly focus "in and outs," because even if I didn't do it, this is the first film where it was photographed under my instructions. I asked the photographer to shoot it that way. And I haven't had time to view all of the footage, un-fortunately. But I have a feeling that it's really groovy. I do know, since the music is so important to my method of cutting, that I have already started conceiving the music for the flower film, even with no idea of what the visuals are.

I want the music to tell me how to cut it. That way, I get the coordination between the music and the visuals. I know that it will be done on a sort of a pseudo-Moog synthesizer. It's done with normal instruments, usually woodwinds, except I plan to get an electrified piano to sound something like a harpsichord. I know that the kind of music will be a mixture of baroque-folk. And I hope to commision either Judy Collins or Joni Mitchell to do a theme song that will be instrumented with this baroque-folk so that there will be a continuity of sound throughout the picture.

The structure will become clear when I view the visuals. That's always practically the first thing that's done.

It is interesting how very few films are scored first. It is a technique that Hollywood is coming to. I read in a journal that some cutter or director or producer, I forget who it was now, said that it should be done more often, and I agree. It is an extremely good way of cutting, but to do it, you've got to have close rapport between the musicians and the composer and the creator of the film. You've got to have a structure beforehand, which is sort of a rough guide. Now everything that I described to Dave Adams when I was talking about the film, I described to the composer beforehand. I develop a structure in my head of the film which is actually not dependent upon the footage except that I have to know what sort of footage I have

got. But it's dependent upon the fact that I think films should have form . . . they should develop. They should have either a very driving beginning or a very slow beginning, one or the other. This turns out to be a slow, lyrical beginning. Actually it should always be that slow—and then get fast, slow, and then punch at the end. *Full Fathom Five,* oddly enough, is very successfully done by going very slow at the end, which is also planned.

I hate to admit to a failing, but since I've never really done a film like this without cutting to music, I'm not sure that my innate sense of rhythm would be up to it. I tried to do *Full Fathom Five* when I had another conception. It changed conceptions three times during the body of the film: once when I was going to do it to this music; once when I decided I wouldn't do it to the music, and then—starting to cut it without the music—and discovered that I was sort of a wash.

I could probably develop the faculty of timing it out myself, but I was afraid that I would never be able to get music that would go with it. So, basically, music might be a crutch, but I feel that it's indispensable to this type of film. It might also be a springboard."

HOME OF THE BRAVE

"On *Home of the Brave,* I made out the exposure sheets for the animation, which means that I didn't quite direct it, even though the director normally does that. Mike Bloebaum who created the film gave me loose instructions on how to do it, but the technique of animation, getting down to the nitty-gritty with the camera and everything, would take too long for him to learn. I know it, so I could do it. My contribution was mostly the colors, which is very tricky. It's more important than it sounds. Colors have a tremendous psychological effect. Maybe the colors won't work out—I haven't seen them. But I thought very hard about colors applying to vi-

suals and interacting with themselves to increase their brightness. Sylvia Dees did the color work on Braverman's films. She has done a lot of research on this subject. She spent years and years in art school and in film and in animation, and probably knows more about the psychological effects of color than anybody in the world, perhaps. She is a very valuable person to know. I learned a lot about that from her."

THE BRAVERMAN FILMS

"My work on the Braverman films was twofold: I organized the material; history is a semi-hobby of mine. I have a pretty good memory, and for some reason, history sticks. The general organization was mine. I also collected all the pictures, doing a good amount of research, especially on *World of '68.* I went through foreign magazines—just every conceivable source that I could think of that was readily available. Because I had done that, even on *World of '68,* where Chuck knew the events that happened, I organized it anyway. Plus things like reading the track and doing a lot of busy-work, which has to be done. I hate to emphasize my contribution to his films, because they were *his* films. Sylvia Dees did a lot of work on them. She shot *World of '68.* I assisted her on that. It's a difficult procedure.

167

Kinestasis is a tool more than technique. The possibilities are immense. It can be used for a lot of different purposes. I think it could be used as one technique in a film filled with other techniques, too. A full kinestasis film has one weakness. The eye gets tremendously fatigued after a short period of time. However, I would like to use it one day, perhaps in a longer film, maybe two or three sequences that are done that way—maybe a two-reeler, or something like that.

Turned On, well, the closest to kinestasis it gets are the da-da-da-da-cuts—those are as short as practically any of the stuff in Chuck's films—five frames, four frames, and he never got below three, except one sequence of two's."

FUTURE PLANS

"My overriding hobby has always been science fiction and space. I would like to do a kinestasis on the dawn of the space age, preferably with lots of NASA stills. I don't know, maybe I can do it. I have never really done a kinestasis—created it, even though I have the knowledge to do it when I feel ready. Maybe that is the next step.

I have found my bag. I really enjoy sitting and doing crossword puzzles in the editing chair. That's how I think of these. I'm putting together into a pattern—it's very much like doing a crossword puzzle, and it has to fit, and it has to flow—especially getting the visuals to move with the music, too. Not just cutting with the music, but getting the back-and-forth motion, or something like that. It's very tricky, but I glory in it. I would like to be a director, be a part of making the films, but I also like the cutting room and perhaps some sort of a combination of the two would be ultimately what I'd like to do.

The content of the music represents the visuals. And it always succeeds. If I have the footage, I will always do it through cutting to music. Occasionally, I know what I need and I know what

I want, but I don't have the visuals to do it, which is the penalty for cutting film that I had nothing to do with putting on film to begin with.

With the flower film, which I think we'll call *Bouquet,* I will at least have some chance. The problem is, what I really should do is have the music done first, then go out and shoot the picture and then cut it. That would be the ideal sequence in making a picture like this."

THE PRODUCER

Lynn and David Adams own Pyramid Films.
There are many impressive things about Lynn
and David—their energy, their enthusiasm, their
high standards, their kindness, their willingness
to take chances—but most impressive of all,
perhaps, is their devotion to excellent filmmaking.

They are certainly not afraid of work. Pyramid
Films is a full-time operation. They frequently
work 18 hours a day—occasionally around the
clock. David studied art before he became a
film producer. His first successful film was *That
They May Live,* a film about mouth-to-mouth
resuscitation that has been seen worldwide and
has saved many lives. He continues to make
films on medical subjects. His current project
is a film called *Life in The Balance,* about cor-
onary care. The author of the book had his first
film-acting experience as a heart patient in this
film. It will probably be his last film-acting role,
too, because he feels his talents may lie outside
the shooting set.

David has been producing films for 11 years.
His films have won many awards and will doubt-
less win many more.

Most mornings, if you want to get up at six
o'clock, you will find Lynn and David jogging
down Ocean Boulevard in Santa Monica. An
independent, shrewd businessman, as well as
an artist, David has managed to keep his head
above water while doing what he enjoys most —
producing works of art that millions enjoy.

PRODUCER'S STATEMENT

I'm often asked, "What, exactly, is the role of a producer?" Sam Goldwyn defines him as someone who: ". . . doesn't write, direct, photograph, act or edit, but without him, pictures would not be created." Of course, this statement applies to the theatrical film producer, but I suppose some of it is also true of the educational or non-theatrical producer. Far removed from Sam Goldwyn's concept is the filmmaker who writes, directs, photographs, acts, composes, plays, narrates, edits, records sound and cuts the negative. With this one-man band effort, he is his own producer.

Compare the film producer with the conductor of a symphony orchestra. The conductor takes the individual talents of the musicians and blends them into a harmonious whole. The film producer "orchestrates" creative talent (both artists and technicians) and ultimately produces a film in which all complement each other. Both the talent and the subject matter are usually selected by the producer. Certainly, he sets the standards and the final quality of the production.

The producer has two other responsibilities. He finances the film, and arranges for its distribution. If the producer does not have his own distribution company, he must select a company that will enhance his image.

Some producers dominate and overshadow the talent to such an extent that each one loses his identity. My own policy is to give maximum latitude and to encourage individuality. This does not imply lack of control or a free-wheeling situation where anything goes. Brain-storming sessions between the producer and the various individuals in a project are very common. In fact, there is an atmosphere of lovely interaction —

what I call "controlled confrontation." This generates enthusiasm, and stimulates the creative process. I would like to think that my strength as a producer lies in esthetic expertise, rather than technical or financial know-how, although probably an amalgamation of all three would be ideal.

Formal training in film can be useful for learning method or technique but it cannot substitute for creativity. The most important requirement in a producer or anyone in film is a visceral feeling for, and a basic faith in the medium itself. By this I do not mean a cerebral or intellectual approach involving the merits of electronic form versus print form, etc. This should be left to experts such as McLuhan and his disciples. Rather, it takes a deep-rooted conviction in the power of film to provide information, enlightenment, motivation, or enrichment.

Print makes it possible for everyone to use the three R's. Film permits what I call the three C's —create, communicate, change.

CREATE

A filmmaker can use his ability to create, explore and innovate in an infinite number of ways. There is no final prescription for creating film.

COMMUNICATE

Once created, film can be experienced in a variety of ways including 8mm, 16mm, 35mm, TV, EVR, Select-a-vision, etc. This versatility gives it a tremendous advantage and impact.

CHANGE

In 1961, McLuhan said, "We have an acceleration of change to the point where the change itself becomes the very matrix and foundation of society." The decade that followed speaks for itself. Film not only reflects the fast changing world, it affects it as well. It can have a powerful impact on the changing of social policies—not always for the betterment of mankind. The students of today must develop a visual literacy in order to make correct value judgments.

Unfortunately, many of the so-called educational films do not take advantage of the three C's. Many are merely lectures on celluloid, or a transfer of the three R's to film. One major company actually uses the trade name 'Text-Films.'

I am happy to be a small part of this change—not only in the films I produce for myself, but in the films I distribute for other producers. *Why Man Creates* by Saul Bass perfectly illustrates the three C's. The thousands of letters from administrators, teachers, students and other people reflect the growing need for more noncurriculum oriented film statements. A teacher in a California high school wrote as follows:

"I am a teacher of history and ethics—in search of an overview to human experience and the past of mankind. An enthused, almost ecstatic parent of one of my students assured me that this new film, *Why Man Creates,* provides such an overview in an exceptional and humorous way."

THE FUTURE

As film becomes more recognized as a language art, its study will become part of the curriculum along with the three R's. Students, even at a kindergarten level, will be supplied with equipment for making films. Many new concepts in hardware—both for production and projection will be developed. Film may never become, as Jean Cocteau and Robert Flaherty predicted, as inexpensive as paper and pencils, but it probably will be as common. What are now considered to be curriculum films will become less popular until they eventually disappear. Films that are now considered supplemental will become the "new" curriculum films.

Ten years ago the average educational film budget for a one-reel film was $3,000. Today's youth watch one-minute TV commercials that cost an average of $30,000. The calibre for films in the classroom will have to become more sophisticated and visually exciting. The National Film Board of Canada has produced some of the finest films in existence, but they were a government-supported institution, and thus not profit-oriented. Although the films are sold commercially, they are subsidized 75 to 90 per cent by the government. The logical thing in this country is for industry to produce or subsidize good educational films not based on the promotion of their products, and identified only by the company's trademark on the end of the film. This would become part of the trend for the entire community to become more interested and actively involved in the educational process.

—*David Adams,* Pyramid Films

HARDWARE

A film production company is people. It's also equipment—hardware as it is sometimes called. Pyramid's hardware includes a 16mm Photo-Sonic camera capable of shooting at speeds up to 400 frames per second. This is the one to take on location if you want to capture ultra slow motion shots of action sports.

If you need some stills for titles or a kinestasis film, check out the Hasselblad, the same make of 2-1/4 x 2-1/4 still camera used by David Hemmings in the movie "Blow Up," and by the astronauts on the moon.

Is your assignment an African Safari? Better take along a 400mm Omnitar lens. It puts your eye, but not your head, close to the tiger's teeth. How about sound? The Nagra tape recorder will give you high fidelity far from electrical outlets. But don't leave it lying around. It costs $1,700, and the batteries are extra. Once your footage is all in the can, you'll appreciate Pyramid's editing equipment: moviolas, bins for your off cuts, splicers, and even a specially designed editing chair.

If you're thinking of starting your own film production company and want to duplicate Pyramid's hardware inventory, be sure you have plenty of cash. About $45,000 should do it—provided you can arrange a good discount.

CAMERAS

2 16mm Arriflex cameras with accessories
1 16mm Bolex Rex camera and lenses
1 Beaulieu camera
1 16mm Photo-Sonic high speed camera
1 Hasselblad 2-1/4 x 2-1/4 still camera
1 Warner 2-1/4 x 2-1/4 still camera
3 Sun Guns
2 Quartz lamps and stands

LENSES

4 16mm 12-120 Angenieux lenses
1 16mm 12-240 Angenieux lens
1 400mm Omnitar lens with cradle and special heavy tripod stand
3 Standard 16mm Cooke lenses
2 Tripods with Miller fluid heads

SOUND EQUIPMENT

1 Nagra tape recorder with Byer microphone
2 Ampex tape recorders with speakers
2 Fisher speakers
1 Uher tape recorder
1 Grundig tape recorder
1 Saxon tape recorder
1 YAMAHA organ synthesizer

PROJECTION EQUIPMENT

2 Bell & Howell 16mm optical sound automatic projectors
2 Kodak 16mm sound projectors
1 Graflex 16mm sound projector
1 35mm optical sound projector
1 Super-8mm sound Technicolor 1000 projector with rear screen
1 2-1/4 x 2-1/4 slide projector
1 35mm Kodak Carousel slide projector
1 Technicolor Super-8mm loop projector
1 Kodak Super-8mm silent projector
1 8 x 10 Electric beaded screen
1 Kodak Daylite screen
9 Deluxe theatre chairs

EDITING EQUIPMENT

2 16mm sound moviolas
1 16mm moviola picture head
4 16mm movie-scopes
8 Editing tables and rewinds
5 Trim bins
5 Synchronizers (various sizes)
4 16mm hot splicers
2 16mm tape splicers
1 35mm hot splicer
1 35mm tape splicer
5 Editing chairs
2 Film racks
5 Luxo lamps

TRANSPORTATION

2 Econo-line camper vans

THE AUTHOR

David A. Sohn is coordinator for English and social studies, Evanston, Illinois. His background in the educational field includes teaching, lecturing and developing reading and study skills programs.

Mr. Sohn has authored, co-authored or edited over a dozen books, including *Stop, Look and Write: Effective Writing Through Pictures, Frost: The Poet and His Poetry, Ten Top Stories, Revolution in Teaching: New Theory, Technology and Curricula, New Directions in Reading, Film Study and The English Teacher,* and *Pictures For Writing.* He recently wrote the film script, *Autumn: Frost Country.* In addition, Mr. Sohn is Contributing Editor for *Media and Methods* magazine and a frequent contributor to other educational publications and professional journals.

In 1967-68, Mr. Sohn served as director of curriculum research with the National Film Study Project at Fordham University; he acted as conference coordinator for the Film Study in the Schools Conference, Washington, D. C., February, 1968.

We'd like to express our thanks to all the filmmakers, producers, and those 'behind the scenes' who supplied us with many photographs and helped with technical information. We especially wish to acknowledge the constant helpfulness of David and Lynn Adams at Pyramid Films who responded to our 'urgent,' 'rush' calls with calm good cheer.

Alan G. Oddie
Marlene A. Shebu
GEO. A. PFLAUM, Publisher
